Ben is a dynamic voice for this con...   r-
rect view of God, this subject will shape more of your life than any .....er.
— **JENNIE ALLEN**, FOUNDER OF IF:GATHERING
AND AUTHOR OF *NOTHING TO PROVE*

Scriptural. Helpful. Standout. In the flurry of conversation around singleness, dating, and marriage, Ben Stuart charts a navigational framework
of Scripture—interwoven with story and statistics—that will help people
of any age chart the often choppy waters of relationships.
— **LOUIE GIGLIO**, PASTOR OF PASSION CITY CHURCH, FOUNDER OF
PASSION CONFERENCES, AND AUTHOR OF *GOLIATH MUST FALL*

Our happiness and health in life are directly proportional to our happiness and health in our relationships. What Ben Stuart shares in this book
might have more influence on your life than anything else you will read
this year.
— **CLAY SCROGGINS**, LEAD PASTOR, NORTH POINT COMMUNITY CHURCH

Ben Stuart has more experience helping young adults discover God's will
and direction for their relationships than anyone I know. Ben will inspire
and equip you to grow through each relationship stage and point you to
God's eternal purposes.
— **CRAIG GROESCHEL**, PASTOR OF LIFE.CHURCH AND AUTHOR OF *FROM*
THIS DAY FORWARD: FIVE COMMITMENTS TO FAIL-PROOF YOUR MARRIAGE

Every bit of life is demarcated by particular features, or characterized
by specific festivities, just like seasons in a year. I've learned that every
demarcation, whether festive or miserable, can be used powerfully by
God. Ben Stuart does an extraordinary job exploring and explaining how.
— **DAVID CROWDER**, RECORDING ARTIST

Ben Stuart has created a masterful relationship handbook for anyone
who wants to get from single to dating to married in a healthy way that
is enjoyable instead of stressful.
— **SHAUNTI FELDHAHN**, SOCIAL RESEARCHER AND BESTSELLING
AUTHOR OF *FOR WOMEN ONLY* AND *FOR MEN ONLY*

Young people today have an increasing challenge when navigating life
from singleness to marriage. Ben Stuart shows us that each season of our

life—singleness to marriage—is connected, and they mean more to God and our life than we realize.

—**CHAD VEACH, LEAD PASTOR OF ZOE CHURCH, LOS ANGELES**

The road map that Ben so brilliantly lays out in these pages will lead you to exactly where your heart truly wants to go. Dive in, friend. It will be worth it!

—**SHANE BARNARD, MUSICIAN, WORSHIP LEADER,**
AND MEMBER OF SHANE & SHANE

In an age when courtship is considered archaic, marriage postponed, and intimacy expected at the mere swipe of the screen, *Single. Dating. Engaged. Married.* is a much-needed anchor for those in the troubled waters of dating and relationships.

—**MARIAN JORDAN ELLIS, AUTHOR OF *SEX AND THE***
SINGLE CHRISTIAN GIRL* AND *STAND

Ben Stuart offers the church a needed primer on pursuing marriage in the modern age.

—**DR. RUSSELL MOORE, PRESIDENT, ETHICS & RELIGIOUS LIBERTY COMMISSION**

Ben masterfully uses Scripture to take us down a path of understanding what God intended for man, woman, and marriage.

—**JONATHAN POKLUDA, TEACHING PASTOR, WATERMARK**
CHURCH, AND LEADER OF THE PORCH, DALLAS, TEXAS

This is an invaluable resource that will help countless young adults maximize joy and minimize unnecessary pain while navigating the various stages of romantic love.

—**TIMOTHY ATEEK, EXECUTIVE DIRECTOR, BREAKAWAY MINISTRIES**

Ben is wise, authentic, humorous, and utterly effective at opening God's Word in ways that transform a soul.

—**KEN WERLEIN, FOUNDING PASTOR, FAITHBRIDGE CHURCH, HOUSTON, TEXAS**

I'm confident that whatever stage of relationship you are in, you will benefit from the wisdom put forth in this book.

—**JAMIE IVEY, AUTHOR OF *IF YOU ONLY KNEW* AND HOST**
OF *THE HAPPY HOUR WITH JAMIE IVEY* PODCAST

Ben Stuart tackles one of history's most complex and confusing subjects with clarity and candor.

—**GREGG MATTE, PASTOR OF HOUSTON'S FIRST BAPTIST**
CHURCH AND AUTHOR OF *UNSTOPPABLE GOSPEL*

ben stuart

single. dating. engaged. married.
navigating **life + love** in the modern age

W PUBLISHING GROUP

AN IMPRINT OF THOMAS NELSON

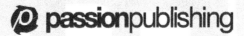

Published in Nashville, Tennessee, by W Publishing, an imprint of Thomas Nelson.

Thomas Nelson titles may be purchased in bulk for educational, business, fundraising, or sales promotional use. For information, please e-mail SpecialMarkets@ ThomasNelson.com.

Unless otherwise noted, Scripture quotations are taken from the ESV® Bible (The Holy Bible, English Standard Version®). Copyright © 2001 by Crossway, a publishing ministry of Good News Publishers. Used by permission. All rights reserved.

Scripture quotations marked MEV are from the Modern English Version. Copyright © 2014 by Military Bible Association. Used by permission. All rights reserved.

Scripture quotations marked NASB are from New American Standard Bible®. Copyright © 1960, 1962, 1963, 1968, 1971, 1972, 1973, 1975, 1977, 1995 by The Lockman Foundation. Used by permission. (www.Lockman.org)

Scripture quotations marked NIV are from the Holy Bible, New International Version®, NIV®. Copyright © 1973, 1978, 1984, 2011 by Biblica, Inc.® Used by permission of Zondervan. All rights reserved worldwide. www.zondervan.com. The "NIV" and "New International Version" are trademarks registered in the United States Patent and Trademark Office by Biblica, Inc.®

Scripture quotations marked NKJV are from the New King James Version®. © 1982 by Thomas Nelson. Used by permission. All rights reserved.

ISBN 978-0-7180-9843-8 (eBook)

Library of Congress Control Number: 2017946407

ISBN 978-0-7180-9789-9 (trade paper)

Printed in the United States of America

HB 07.02.2024

contents

To my beloved bride, Donna.
The fire in my heart and light in my eyes.
Let's run this race forever.

introduction

Texas A&M University possesses a unique culture. It combines the traditions of a rich military history with the earthiness of agricultural and mechanical schools, anchored with a whole lot of we-can-do-it-because-we're-from-Texas attitude. I loved going to college there, though, admittedly, when I arrived as a freshman I knew surprisingly little about the school.

So I will never forget the first time I entered the football stadium, Kyle Field. The football game did not start until the next day. Yet my roommates and I joined the throng of more than ten thousand of our fellow classmates as we entered the stadium a few minutes before midnight.

As an inexperienced freshman, I peppered my upperclassmen roommates with questions like, "So what is this we're doing? Why are we here at midnight?" They explained that the student body always gathered the night before games in order to practice the yells that we would all be shouting in unison the following day. Like I said: unique. But it had a certain logic to it. A crowd of thousands all yelling the exact same well-rehearsed chant throughout the game had proven to be a successful tactic to intimidate and confuse opposing teams.

But then my roommates' explanations took a strange turn. They continued, "So we will practice the yells for a few minutes, and then, at a certain moment, all the lights will be turned out and *we will all make out with the person standing next to us.*"

"Wait. What?!"

"When the lights go out you kiss the girl you brought," they explained. "Or, if you didn't bring someone, don't worry. You hold up a lighter, and someone will find you and you will make out with them." I laughed for a moment, but quickly ceased when I realized they were not joking.

Suddenly, a wave of anxiety swept over me. This was an introvert's nightmare.

What am I supposed to do?

I didn't bring a date.

Am I really going to kiss a random person?

What if no one finds me?

What if someone does and I really don't want to kiss them? Do I cough? Act like I'm sick? Hit the ground? What does any of this have to do with football?!

In the end I admitted to myself that I wasn't ready for this kind of pressure. I think I shook my roommates' hands and then stared at my shoes until the moment was over.

But I remember in that moment how it struck me as fascinating that the simple act of turning off the lights could instantly create such a variety of strong emotional responses around the stadium. For some this would be thrilling. They came with someone cute they had just started dating, or with whom they felt there was some potential, and this was going to be an epic moment in their relationship. For others this would just be business as usual. They had been dating for fourteen years, which isn't even right, but we all know those people who show up to college and they're already like an old couple. They'd simply kiss like they always do, with most of the thrill gone. For others the extinguishing of the lights at this Midnight Yell suddenly flooded back the memories of the person they kissed at the last one, who was now gone. And that simple act of turning off the lights brought up a torrent of pain. Maybe for others that moment when the stadium went dark was yet another reminder of how they have always been so desperately alone. Or, like me, maybe it brought a rush of competing anxieties: the fear of being alone crashing into the fear of being in a relationship, creating a tsunami of panic.

Why mention this Texas A&M experience? Because in the same way that all those varied emotional responses were ignited with the flip of a switch at a college football tradition, I have found this very phenomena occurs in any room full of single people when you say the word *dating*. Though I have stood in stadiums full of college students who cheered when I announced from stage, "We will be talking about relationships," I have also stood before rooms full of mid-to-late twentysomethings who groaned audibly when they heard the same sentence. Why such a disparity of responses from people relatively the same age?

For some the thought of dating conjures up all manner of stress because they feel so much uncertainty about how to do it. Over the years I have had hundreds of conversations with young people who ask me questions like, "What am I supposed to do if I am interested in somebody? What are the rules now? Do I call them? Will they think that's weird? Who calls anymore? So am I supposed to try to corner her somewhere and tell her I think she's pretty? That feels really stalker-ish! Do I just comment on their social media a lot? Should I send a private message, or is that trying to create a secret world too fast? Should I text? Is that too informal? Do I try to stay casual and say, 'Let's go hang out'? Or is that not clear and intentional enough? Should I ask them to go on a 'date' with me? Is that too formal, too old-school? What are the rules?!" For many young people the topic of dating creates little thrill. It mainly produces anxiety.

For others, dating is their absolute favorite topic to talk about. When the word comes to mind she thinks about the cute guy who did text. Her thoughts drift back to that moment when she saw his name flash onto the screen of her phone, sending a message asking if it'd be possible to go to dinner. She recalls with fond affection the moment she showed the text to her friends, and collectively all their adrenaline spiked and the comments began to fly: "He texted you! I told you he likes you! What are you going to say? Say yes! You'll make such a cute couple. Your name goes great with his last name." Or, you are the guy who sent the text and felt your heart pound as you waited for her reply. After an agonizing few seconds you felt the deep satisfaction of success when you saw the response come in that she'd love to spend time with you. Smiling to yourself you dropped the phone and whispered, "Pay attention, world. A master is at work. Say my name!" For some the topic of dating brings a rush of positive emotions because you know the thrill of being interested in someone and discovering that they like you too.

Yet, for others, when they think about relationships it does not conjure feelings of anxiety or anticipation, but those of agony. A few years ago at Breakaway, the ministry I led on the campus of Texas A&M, we held a worship service for thousands of college students at Kyle Field. I was addressing the toxic nature of secrets, how they can sap our energy and steal our joy. Though I challenged them to talk to a trusted peer or mentor about the things that were eating them up on the inside, I encouraged them, as a first step, to write down some of their secrets on a piece of paper and drop them in bins we had down near the track. Thousands came forward. Over the next few days my team and I read through the cards, praying for the students who wanted to release the burden of guilt and shame that they were already carrying at such a young age. What I saw surprised even me. Maybe three or four out of every five cards addressed the deep hurt and desperate heartbreak that accompanied a romantic relationship that had gone wrong. Some expressed regret over a relationship that they had stayed in too long. Others lamented giving away too much of themselves emotionally or physically to someone who was not worthy of their affections. Others expressed remorse over betraying trusts. The sheer volume of relational pain expressed in this mountain of confessions was overwhelming. Over my years in ministry among young people, I can tell you, nobody cries like the brokenhearted. The impulse within us to pair off into relationships is good, even powerful. But when it goes poorly, the decoupling can be intensely painful.

So if pairing off is both desirable and dangerous, how do we do it right? Before we delve into any advice about what to do, we need to figure out where we are. Surveying the lay of the land will help us in our attempts to navigate the complexities of life and love in modern times. So let's begin with a few things we do know.

First, the vast majority of young people want to get married. The most rigorous and reliable surveys available today put the number in the high 90th percentile. So the rumors of the death of marriage have been greatly exaggerated.[1]

Second, the vast majority of young people today will get married. Not only will they marry, the majority of them will do so in their twenties. In 2012, 80 percent of Americans over the age of twenty-five were, or had been, married. That's four out of every five.[2] An additional 13 percent, while not married, were said to be living with a long-term partner. While there are important shifts in our culture today regarding when, and if, to get married, the reality is most people on the planet want to be married and will be married.[3] So if you are a college student reading this, you will most likely pass through the distinct life phases of singleness, dating, engagement, and marriage all within a single decade. In these two areas—the desire to get married and the likelihood of marriage in your future—you are not too unlike the generations that have come before you.

Yet, there is one way young people today are different than their predecessors. They are waiting longer to get married than any other generation in recorded history. Today, the average age for a young woman getting married is twenty-seven. For young men it is twenty-nine.[4] To put that in perspective, in the 1990s, the average age a woman got married was twenty-three. Men married around age twenty-six.[5] This is a significant shift in just the last couple of decades, which raises an important question. Why, if the majority of young people want to get married, are they waiting so long to do so?

As is often the case, there is not one simple answer. Instead, there are a variety of reasons, some of which may resonate with you more than others.

First is the fear of divorce. Many young people witnessed their parents' divorce and still feel the pain it caused.[6] In response they have vowed not to rush into marriage and risk making the same mistake.[7]

Others do not fear that they will mess up marriage, but that marriage will mess them up! In the past, marriage used to be viewed as the first step into adulthood. Now it is the last step. Believing a covenant relationship may interfere with their career goals, they choose professional impact now and defer personal intimacy until later.[8]

Confusion arising from modern forms of communication plays a role in the delay in marriage as well. The rapid rise of technology has created several means of connecting with other people. Unfortunately, this has complicated the script of how to initiate romantic conversation. In the past, if someone wanted to ask another person on a date, he would call them. Today, many young people find that odd. Some believe it is more polite to text. Others think that is too informal. The lack of clarity in the prescribed dating scripts has actually slowed down the dating process.

Others become paralyzed by the endless dating options now available. A study conducted in Philadelphia revealed that in 1932 a whopping one-third of all couples lived within a five-block radius of each other before they got married. Only 17.8 percent were from different cities.[9] Today young people can get online and interact with people all over the globe. Dating apps have made the pool of potential mates massive, which has resulted in young people slowing down their willingness to commit to a single individual. *How sure am I that someone better won't come along, when I see thousands of potential mates on my phone every day?*

Compounding this stress is the pressure to find a "soul mate." By this I mean the growing impulse to look for far more than a companion in life. *I want someone who will fill every vacancy in me, awaken dormant gifts inside, and continuously enrapture me in other-worldly emotional bliss.* This puts tremendous pressure on another human being.[10]

For others progress to marriage is impeded by seeking the fulfillment of sexual desires outside of a relationship. In the past sexual desire served as a drive to propel people into marriage because marriage was the safest and most acceptable place to have sex. Now society has largely removed any taboo associated with premarital sex. Additionally, the meteoric rise in accessibility to pornography has offered an avenue for acting out sexually that has, for many, replaced even the search for a human partner. Now that sex can be had anywhere, it has eliminated a strong motivator that aimed young people toward covenant relationship with another human being.[11]

As I researched all these factors contributing to the delay of marriage, I continued to ask the question, "What is underneath all of this? What motives are driving these trends?" When I contemplate the landscape of life and love for young people today, in many people I see *fear*. Fear of making a mistake. Fear of missing out. Fear of losing opportunities. I see so much fear in the hearts of young men and women. In others I hear *pride*. The insistence to live life on your own terms so that no one can threaten your freedom of expression. In many I also see *lust*. Why commit to love someone emotionally if I can just use them physically? Fear, pride, and lust are the root of so many problems I see cropping up in relationships.

When I see these, it makes sense why lifelong love is being delayed. None of these drivers aim at love. Love opens up and gives of itself freely. Fear closes off and withdraws. Love risks vulnerability for the sake of the beloved. Pride will not tolerate the risk of self for the other. Love embraces all of a person, on their best days and their worst. Lust says I only want the parts of you I can use. As long as fear, lust, and pride are in the driver's seat, the culture will be speeding away from healthy love. And we *are already* seeing it in the culture. We are not headed in healthy directions.

For the first time in the history of the United States, the average age a woman has her first child is younger than the average age of a woman entering her first marriage. On average, women in America are having their first child at age twenty-six. The average American woman gets married at age twenty-seven.[12] This is historic. More than 40 percent of children born in our country today are born to unwed mothers.[13] This concerns me because studies show that on every measurable scale children are worse off when they lack the opportunity to grow up in a home with a loving father and mother.

From 2005 to 2012 one-third of all couples who got married in

America met on a dating site. I am not going to bash dating websites. I have friends who met and fell in love with their spouses online. But what does concern me is that each new online dating portal tends to move more and more toward analyzing a person based on the one aspect of them that is sure to fade: physical beauty. This does not make for the wisest criteria for compatibility or successful and enduring marriages.

The Centers for Disease Control and Prevention issued a statement recently explaining that since the advent of Tinder and other dating apps that promote "date" selection based primarily on physical beauty, they have seen a skyrocketing increase in sexually transmitted diseases. In 2015 in Rhode Island, since the advent of Tinder and Grindr, syphilis cases have risen 79 percent. Gonorrhea and HIV have increased by more than 30 percent.[14]

Studies have also shown a significant increase in self-reported loneliness and depression in college students today compared to previous generations.[15] And in the midst of the loss of the intimacy found in marriage, addiction has risen to take its place.[16]

Why mention all of this? Because for all of our connectivity through technology, we have suffered a loss of community. Fear, pride, and lust are driving us into isolation or creating shallow relationships that do not serve human flourishing.

You may be asking, "What are you advocating, Ben? That we paddle back to some bygone era that was supposedly amazing where everyone got married when they were thirteen, had kids at fourteen, then milked the goats, churned butter, and built barns until they died at thirty?" No. I don't have any misty-eyed, glowing view of some bygone era. There is no former port that I am trying to sail us back to.

But that doesn't change the fact that when I look at us today I see a generation lost at sea, unsure how to navigate the increasingly tempestuous sea of life and love. We are adrift, battered by the winds and waves of these modern times. The good news, however, is that in the midst of uncertain seas, we do have a way to chart a course forward.

Several years ago a man by the name of Steve Callahan was lost at sea—after a terrible boating accident—in a little rubber raft for seventy-six days somewhere between Africa and the Caribbean. Though he was emaciated and dazed, he managed to take three pencils and lash them together to create a sextant—a navigational tool that allows you to use the horizon and the sun to get your bearings. Based on his application of these nautical realities, he was able to discern the latitude, catch the right current, and drift safely to the Caribbean. It was his understanding of fixed realities in the universe that helped him navigate his environment successfully. We have an opportunity to do the same. In the midst of uncertain relational seas, we, too, can look up and find our bearings by understanding the unchanging realities of who God is and what he is doing in the world.

That is why I wrote this book. I earnestly hope that these pages can give you clarity in relational uncertainty. In the pages that follow, we will focus on four distinct relational stages that the vast majority of human beings will pass through at some point in their lives: singleness, dating, engagement, and marriage. Each stage has a God-given purpose that you can either choose to embrace and fulfill, or not. Each stage also has some advantages and disadvantages that are distinct. We will identify the God-given purpose for each stage—the guiding stars we will navigate by. We will also identify and maximize the advantages of each stage and identify and minimize the unique challenges of each stage. I want to give you fixed points to navigate by, so you can sail on into the unknown with the confidence of knowing that whatever relational stage you are in, your life can be lived with an incredible sense of purpose. Let's be clear from the outset: this journey does not start with you identifying a cute person who has some potential. You do not need romantic interest to discover your life's purpose. Your journey begins with your Maker.

Back in the day, when a ship sailed into treacherous waters, often the captain had to acknowledge that he lacked the sufficient knowledge of the area to guide his vessel safely into port through the dangerous rocks and shoals. When that realization came upon a captain, before the days of modern communication, he would raise a flag that signaled to all around "I require a pilot." When that flag ascended the mast, a pilot familiar with the area would jump into his little coracle, row out to the ship, and come aboard. The pilot would then commandeer the vessel and guide it safely through the uncertain seas. To signal to other pilots who may want to come aboard that they were not needed, the vessel would then fly another flag, one that was half red and half white. The flag declared to all who cared to see, "I have a pilot." No other pilots were needed, and the locals could be assured that this ship was in safe hands.

Are you willing to admit the same need?

In the unpredictable waters of love, we need a guide. Someone familiar with the area. Someone who can navigate us away from the dangers hidden just under the surface that could shipwreck us. One that could lead us safely to shore. The good news is that we need not sail alone. The God who made you and every other human being on the planet can guide you safely home. The Bible tells us that God is love. Do you want a reliable guide in the unknown waves of love? Admit your need. Raise your flag and declare to God that you need him to take the wheel and guide you.

This is where our journey must begin.

Ben Stuart
Summer, 2017

first things first

We must get a relationship with God right before we can get a relationship with a guy or a girl right.

1

god, guys, & girls

Beloved, let us love one another, for love
is from God, and whoever loves has
been born of God and knows God.
—1 John 4:7

Several years ago a friend of mine went scuba diving in the Caribbean with some friends and family. They did one of those crazy-unsafe deals where you get an hour or so crash course on all things scuba, then swim out into the ocean. Before the dive she was paired up with a middle-aged man. They were to be scuba buddies—able to function independently, both had their scuba masks and oxygen tanks, but paired up to enjoy the adventure together and to provide support should something go wrong.

As long as they both had their scuba tanks on, air flowing, they were a real source of life for each other—enjoying the wonders of the ocean together. But then something went wrong with his gear. Oxygen ceased flowing. Panic set in. They knew the emergency protocol—a series of hand gestures, sharing of oxygen, then a slow, calm ascent to the boat above. But as soon as he realized he could not breathe, all of that went out the window. He quickly grabbed her by the shoulders, shaking her and trying to yell. She tried to understand what he was doing but none of this looked like the emergency drill they had just learned! As she tried to calm him down, he suddenly yanked her aspirator out of her mouth. Desperation set in. Where there is scarcity, there's desperation. And where there is desperation, there is exploitation. As he struggled for air, he began to push her head down, almost as though he was trying to climb her like a ladder to safety. Of course, what he was actually doing was drowning her. In return she struggled violently with him in order to get the aspirator back and take a breath. Then, in a final act of desperation, he grabbed her and swam full speed toward the surface. In doing so, he forgot to pause and adjust the pressure, so when they arrived at the top they both got decompression sickness, also known as "the bends." They survived but, needless to say, they are no longer swimming buddies, or any kind of buddies for that matter.

The same principle holds true in all of life. When you have a source of life, you are a source of life. But where there is scarcity, desperation will set in. And desperation can easily become exploitation of others. If you are disconnected from a source of life, your "oxygen tank," then you will attempt to suck life out of someone else. You will be tempted to use people to try to get your sense of self validated. You will, in a moment, become a sucker of life rather than a giver of life. And this is how toxic relationships are born. This is why so many go wrong. When we bring God-sized needs to human beings, they cannot possibly succeed. Nor can we offer them unconditional love on the days they are struggling, because they are our source![1]

If it feels like I am painting this in too dark of colors, let me show it to you in the "innocent" way I discovered it in me. When I was in college I yearned for a relationship with a woman. But I remember when I heard someone talk about how husbands sacrifice their wants and desires for the sake of their wives. This person spoke about how Jesus Christ had sacrificed his very life for the sake of his bride, the church. All of this sounded so heroic. I wanted to be a hero like that, so it seemed good to me. But then he talked about how sex is not the using of a person to meet your needs. The same logic applies. What a wife will need in sexually intimate moments will probably not look at all like what a young

> # When you have a source of life, you are a source of life.

guy in his twenties imagines, particularly if he has grown up looking at porn. It was here that my selfishness was exposed. I had always imagined that sex was about gratifying me. I had thought about that aspect of a relationship purely in selfish, self-gratifying terms. I realized that there wasn't much love in my imagery of sex. From there I began to see how in many of my imaginings about romance and marriage, I envisioned me doing things that would make my wife, or others, think that I was heroic, impressive, caring, or otherwise amazing. The endgame was about me. It was an attempt to fill up my ego. I remember weeping thinking about how much selfishness had shot through every aspect of my imagination as it related to romance. I had to take a break from even thinking about a relationship with a girl. I realized I would be looking to her to make me feel as though I was somebody special. Sure, wives should make a husband feel that way, but if I bring a God-sized need for love and acceptance to any girl, no matter how impressive she is, she can't meet a need like that.

We must get a relationship with God right before we will ever get a relationship with a guy or a girl right.

As we look at the Bible, there are certainly a number of sections that address romance, sex, and marriage. We watch the first couple meet in the book of Genesis. We have the romantic songs of Solomon. We have the wise counsel concerning love in the Proverbs. The first letter to the Corinthians addresses single life. Ephesians and Colossians both contain beautiful descriptions of godly marriages. Yet if you were to add up all of these they would constitute only a small sliver of the content of the Word of God. The vast majority of the Scriptures cover the importance of a relationship *with God*. For some young singles I have visited with, this fact can seem hard to imagine. Dating is the largest issue in their view. *What possibly could take precedence over finding the love of your life?* I admit, when the desire to date is as close to you as your nose, it looks all-consumingly large. Yet if you can back up from the desire to date for a moment, you will see that there is a greater story playing out in history than the story of romantic love. Your relationship with a guy or a girl, though important, is not the most critical relationship in your life, and it is not the relationship that God is the most concerned with.

In chapter 4 of the gospel of John, when Jesus sat down with the woman at the well, he struck up a conversation with her about thirst and water. Then, in the context of this conversation about thirst, he said to her, "You have had five husbands and the man you are living with now is not your husband." He also said to her, "If you knew who it was speaking to you, you would have asked me, and I would give you living water." What Jesus was saying to this woman was, "You have been looking for satisfaction for a deep soul thirst in the arms of men and you cannot find it there. You have misdiagnosed your need." Many of us have done the same.

Before you seek a guy or a girl, you need to get on board with God. Before you marry a mate, you need to meet your Maker, because it's in the stability of walking with him that we have the resources to be a blessing to one another. We have to be connected to a source of life if we are going to be a source of life.

In 1 John 4, as John was talking to us about love, he said, "Beloved, let us love one another" (v. 7). He then moved on to give his readers motivation for why they should care for others. But in a fascinating twist, he did not motivate with a threat of punishment or a promise of reward! He did not say, "Love, or else God will be really mad at you!" There is no threat. He also did not say, "Love, because then you'll be blessed with great wealth." There is no future reward in view in the verse. So how did he motivate them? He did not point forward, but backward! He said, "Beloved, let us love one another, for love is from God, and whoever loves has been born of God and knows God. Anyone who does not love does not know God, because God is love" (1 John 4:7–8). He did not point downstream to a promise or threat. He pointed upstream. Love! Why, John? Because love flows down to you from God. And when you know him, it is the most natural thing in the world to let that love flow from him, to you, and on to others. When you know you are "beloved," it is easy to love others. When you have an inexhaustible resource of love, it is easy to be a source of love for others.

Do you want to be a great lover of people? Do you want to be a source of life to your family, friends, anyone who you might date, and the person you will eventually marry? Then you need a source of life. This is how it was always meant to be. The beloved love. Love embraced becomes love extended. It is the natural outworking of being loved by God.

Some of you may say, "How do I feel loved by God? I want to feel loved. How do I feel it?" Let me declare a simple principle: our affection burns off the fuel of truth. If we want to feel loved, then we must begin with knowing that we truly are loved.

So let's take this out of the spiritual world for a moment. How do you know that you are loved by anyone? You can't see love. You can't hold it. What have you got there? "A little cup of love." It doesn't work that way. So how do you know love is truly present in a relationship? You might say to me, "Ben, love is like the wind. You cannot see it, but you feel its effects." And you would be right!

Though love is invisible, it is not imperceptible. Think about your favorite novels or movies. When a writer or director wants to show you that love exists between two characters, what is written into the story? I would submit to you there are three primary ways they show us that love is present.

First, love *sends*. It cannot sit still. Love moves. Love expresses itself in action. You know that love is present because the lover initiates. In the movie *The Princess Bride* the beautiful Princess Buttercup declares to her captors, "I know my Westley will come for me." How does she know? Because what they shared was "true love." The princess understood that the lover always moves to be with the beloved! Love initiates. Love sparks up conversations. Love breaks into song. Love writes poetry. Love sends letters. Buys flowers. Crosses oceans. I promise you, you will never see a young man after suddenly realizing he loves a young woman return to playing a video game. He will rise from that couch and move. Why? Because love initiates.

Second, love *sacrifices*. Love gives all for the sake of the beloved. Jack will freeze to death in the icy waters of the Atlantic in order to save Rose from the sinking *Titanic*. In *Frozen*, Anna will throw herself in front of Hans's falling sword in order to save her sister Elsa. Bruno Mars declares that he would catch an explosive device for you. Why does he sing that? Because he knows that we know that true love will sacrifice itself for the beloved.

Third, love *stays*. Love delights in the presence of the beloved. And love will stay, even when the staying is hard. We declare this in our wedding vows: "I promise to love you for better or for worse, richer or poorer, in sickness and in health." Why do we say this? Because we understand that true love willingly commits to stay with the beloved, even if life gets really complicated. This is why in the movie *The Notebook*, Noah stays long hours at the nursing home to read to Allie even though she has Alzheimer's disease and can't remember who he is. In *50 First Dates* Adam Sandler's character will continue to romance Drew Barrymore's character every day, even though her short-term memory loss means she forgets him every morning and he must start all over again. True love stays even when it is hard. True love stays when everyone else walks out.

Love sends. Love sacrifices. Love stays. Movies and novels will continue to illustrate these attributes of love because we all know that when we see these activities, love is present.

You may be wondering, *What does any of this have to do with whether or not I feel loved by God?*

Don't miss this part.

Love Sends

In 1 John 4:9 John told us, "In this the love of God was made manifest among us." The word *manifest* means "brought into the light." John declared that when we saw something, it suddenly revealed to us that we were loved by God. What was it?

> ". . . that God sent his only Son into the world, so that we might live through him." (1 John 4:9)

God did not send a note. A song. A list of to-dos. He sent his best. He sent his Son. You do not get better. You do not get a more precious emissary. There was no greater person God could have sent.

And notice when God did this the distinction John made: "In this is love, not that we have loved God but that he loved us" (1 John 4:10). God did not wait until we were worthy before he sought us out. He didn't wait until we were organized, sanitized, religious, moral, or good. He came while we were "far off," "enemies," "not seeking," "not interested," and "hostile." How do you know you are loved by God? Because "God so loved the world, that he gave his only Son, that whoever believes in him should not perish but have eternal life" (John 3:16). The historic appearance of Jesus Christ in the world is exhibit A of God's love for you.

Love Sacrifices

Not only did he come for us, he sacrificed for us. John explained that God "loved us and sent his Son to be the propitiation for our sins" (1 John 4:10). The word *propitiation* carries the imagery of the temple in the Old Testament. An innocent lamb was sacrificed in order to cover the guilt of the people. Here John declared that Jesus' death on the cross fulfilled that Old Testament picture.

In my conversations with people from all manner of backgrounds and experiences, I've found most sense that they are not what they should be. Even the least religious people I have met sense within that there is something wrong with them. They feel a weight. A guilt. The question then becomes, "How do I feel okay? How do I feel right with the universe? With God? With myself?" John declared that Jesus took on our guilt, absorbed our shortcomings, and paid for them. He resolved them. He opened up the way for us to have peace with God. God's love propelled him to sacrifice whatever it took so that we could be fully who we were meant to be under God. Many people wonder what they need to do to feel okay. Here John declared that Jesus has done it for us. The weight of your guilt and shame does not need to sink you into the grave. Jesus took your guilt and shame and mine to the grave for us, and conquered it because that's what love does.

In my early twenties I had a roommate who was meticulous with his finances. He kept every receipt. He monitored his spending patterns with detailed spreadsheets. Honestly, I had never seen anything like it for someone under forty. Around that same time he fell in love with a young woman, and the prospect of marriage stood in the not-too-distant future. There was only one problem: through irresponsible spending habits in college, she had racked up a mountain of credit card debt. I could tell that shame threatened to extinguish all the thrill of potential engagement for her. *How could I bring such a burden into a relationship? How could I ask someone to take on the responsibility of paying all this debt that is the direct result of the poor decisions I made?* She also had a difficult family situation. Like, we-will-need-to-hire-security-at-the-wedding difficult. To her it seemed like far too much to ask for someone to take on. I watched my roommate count the cost: it would devastate his credit score. It would take years to repay. It would require navigating complicated family matters, potentially for the rest of their lives. But then I watched him consider this woman. And I remember watching him make the decision: I want to be with her. And if I have to pay a steep cost—I will gladly pay it. He never held it over her head or reminded her of it either. He just stood at that altar beaming on the day of their wedding. Gladly paying the cost to be with his beloved. Because that is what love does. Love sacrifices.

How do you know you are loved by God? Jesus Christ left heaven. Abandoned the prestige. Relinquished all comforts. Lived the life of a poor man. Took the form of a servant. And then sacrificed his life so that we could be forgiven, made clean, and brought into the family of God. Jesus himself declared, "Greater love has no one than this, that someone lay down his life for his friends" (John 15:13). And that is exactly what he did! There is no more he could give.

In 2016 Sally Monsoor christened the largest, most sophisticated destroyer in the United States Navy. The 610-foot, 15,000-ton vessel was named the USS *Monsoor*, in honor of her son, Michael. Ten years prior, Michael Monsoor's Navy SEAL Team was tasked with rooting out enemy fighters from Ramadi, Iraq. While in a sniper position with two other SEALs, a grenade was suddenly lobbed into their midst. Without hesitation, Michael leapt upon the grenade, absorbing the blast and, in doing so, saving his teammates. When President Bush posthumously presented him the Medal of Honor, a teammate said during the speech, "Mikey looked death in the face that day and said, 'You cannot take my brothers. I will go in their stead.'"[2] This is why the United States government presented him with the highest honor, and the navy wants to sail on a ship emblazoned with his name. Because he paid the ultimate sacrifice. And he did it out of love.

> Love embraced becomes love extended.

Now, let me ask you a serious question: Those men on that roof with Michael that day, do you think they ever question whether or not he cared about them? Do you think they wonder at times if he really treasured them? I don't think so. His sacrifice silences any voice of doubt in a moment. He gave all that they might live. That is the ultimate sign of love.

My friend, do you question if Jesus loves you? Do you wonder if heaven smiles down on you or frowns? Look to the cross. See Jesus flinging himself into harm's way on your behalf, absorbing the fatal consequences of our sin and shame so that we might live. You are loved. If you entrust your life to the Son of God, then heaven smiles on you today and always. You live under God's mercy, not judgment.

Love Stays

The final way we can know we are loved: God's love abides with us because his very Spirit has made a home in us. First John 4:13 states, "By this we know that we abide in him and he in us, because he has given us of his Spirit." How do we know that we are loved? Because when God invites us into his family, he never lets go. He puts his very Spirit in us. His love stays.

My senior year in high school I met the most attractive couple I had ever seen in my life. He was a pro athlete. She was a model. And together they were so stunning that when they walked into a room, instantly conversations ceased and heads turned. They were also extraordinarily kind and generous people, which made them easy to root for. They were the all-American couple. Then, as they neared marriage, she was diagnosed with multiple sclerosis. She began to have trouble using her hands. Within a few months, she was unable to lift her arms high enough to brush her own hair. Her condition was worsening without signs of improvement. Seeing a bleak prospect for herself, she pulled her fiancé aside and told him that it was okay if he wanted to call off the engagement. She did not want him to feel bound to someone who would face such difficulty and struggle. He did not consider her offer for a second. I remember sitting in the crowd as they recited their vows to each other. Her eyes welled with tears and her voice cracked as she tried to repeat the words "in sickness and in health." She knew what those words would cost him. He simply smiled back and gripped her hand tightly. He recited his vows with boldness and clarity: "I promise to love you for better or for worse, in sickness and in health until death do us part." He willingly shouldered whatever inconveniences may come, because he wanted to be with his beloved.

God is the same way with us. That word *abide* in 1 John 4 simply means "to stay right here." He knows we will struggle in this life. We will falter and fail. We will be weak. But no matter what comes, his love declares, "I am not leaving. I am staying with you." Because that is what love does. Love stays.

If you are in Christ, the most beautiful and powerful being in existence cherishes you. He knows your name. He sees you. He gave all to make you his. He will never give up on you. You do not need to spend a single moment of your life trying to earn the love or esteem of others. You have his. You do not need to look for anyone to fill up your tank of love. You can find an abundance in him.

When we understand this, when we rest in his loving care, we have the resource within us to enter the world as givers rather than takers. We can be fountains rather than drains. We can use our gifts and resources to bless others rather than use others to try to make us feel blessed. Love embraced becomes love extended. This is the kind of life you want to live in the world!

For the Love of NASCAR

Several years ago a friend of mine invited me to join him and his fiancée at a NASCAR race. On the way to the track, my friend's fiancée, Rebecca, explained that we had a few extra tickets. A few hundred extra to be exact. Instantly upon hearing the news the boys in the car leapt with excitement: "We can sell them!

This is going to be amazing! We'll be rich!" But Rebecca quickly interjected, "Guys, these tickets were freely given to us. I think we should give them away for free." Aw, man. As soon as she said it we realized we probably had to do what she said. It sounded kinda like the Bible. But we weren't super excited about it. Until we got there. When we arrived we encountered a massive line extended from the gate of the track off into the distance of the RV park. The people in line looked anxious. They were hoping to buy tickets to the race, but there was no guarantee they were going to make it in. Rebecca approached a young family in the middle of the line and handed them each a ticket. For a few moments they just stared at her with obvious skepticism. Eventually one of their children ran up to the gate. The track official scanned the ticket, and the child went through. When his parents saw that the tickets worked, they looked up at Rebecca in disbelief. How could you do this? Why would you do this? This is too good to be true! As soon as we saw the look on their faces, all thoughts of making a financial profit fled from our minds. For the next several minutes, all four of us walked up and down the line, discreetly handing out tickets. People laughed. Some cried. It felt amazing to absolutely make their day. Then, when all the tickets were handed out, we used our tickets and went in. As we entered the section to our seats we realized what should have been obvious to us: the tickets we had given away were all in a block of seats. All the people we had given tickets to were seated around us. The next few hours were a blast as we sat amongst all those we had ushered into NASCAR. Why did we experience this joyful moment? What allowed us to be so generous with these tickets? When we knew we had an abundance, we were liberated to be generous.

My friend, it is the same with love. When we know we are connected to the inexhaustible acceptance, forgiveness, grace, and care of the God of the universe, then we are free to extend that same love to all who are in need. This is the kind of person you want to be. This is the kind of husband or wife you want to be. Freely receiving divine love. Freely giving divine love. First John 4:19 declares that "We love because he first loved us." Do you want to be a great friend? A great coworker? A great husband or wife? Then receive the love of God and you will have an abundance to give.

single: devotion

God has ordained a season of singleness for every human being on the planet. Singleness does not exist simply as an extended adolescence, a pursuit of career ambition, or a preparatory phase for marriage. Rather, God has ordained the unique freedoms of single life not for distractions or ambitions, but for devotion to him.

2

the purpose of singleness

I wish that all were as I myself am. But
each has his own gift from God, one
of one kind and one of another.
—1 Corinthians 7:7

When I was young, Christmas always involved extensive travel for my family. We awoke Christmas morning at Mom's house, and then, later that day, would drive down to Beeville, Texas, to visit "Country Grandma's" house. Shortly thereafter we would head north about an hour and a half to San Antonio and visit "City Grandma's" house. We called it the love triangle, driving all around Texas every Christmas.

The best presents were always at my mom's house. That's where Santa came. Country Grandma's gifts were usually a bit odd. White sweatshirts with a big deer on them were common. City Grandma's gifts were always much better. Toys, electronics, stuff like that. Except for one year when it all got flipped.

Country Grandma gave me a slingshot. When I say slingshot

I don't mean a little piece of wood with a rubber band on it. This thing was made of titanium. It had a drop-down forearm grip for maximum leverage and surgical tubing for the sling. It also came with a package of steel balls with pictures on it of the small woodland creatures they expected you to kill with this weapon. I was stunned. My brother and I threw on our deer sweatshirts and raced out the back door to try this baby out. It could break fence boards. It was unbelievable. A Christmas miracle.

As we drove away, I remember thinking, *If Country Grandma is giving out gifts this good, I can't wait to see what City Grandma has in store!* So you can imagine my surprise when City Grandma handed me a single sheet of paper that read "You are the recipient of one hundred shares of stock in such and such company." *Wait. . . . what?*

As I stared in disbelief at this sentence, I think the adults sensed that I was a bit underwhelmed by Grandma's choice of a gift. So they attempted to explain, "Well, Ben, you see, stock is kind of like money, but you can't spend it. But maybe, many years from now, it'll be worth more money." I muttered something like, "Well, we all hope so, don't we?" But inside I was shocked that City Grandma could be so completely clueless. *Why would she waste our time with something as meaningless as this?*

Fast-forward to a couple of years later. I'm playing in the backyard with my friends. My brother, who was grounded at the time, somehow had possession of my slingshot. Suddenly, coming from the direction of his bedroom, pennies started zooming by and one of them hit my arm and drew blood. Money cut into my skin. This unprovoked attack got him in even more trouble, and my slingshot was returned to me. I took it and went to blow off steam by breaking some fence boards. Suddenly the surgical tubing snapped in two, whipping back and cutting my other arm. I remember looking at my bloodied arms in disbelief. How could this happen? This gift, which was supposed to bring me such joy, had brought me nothing but sadness and pain.

Fast-forward again another twenty years later, to the day I arrived on campus for my first day of seminary. I remember entering the student center and seeing a massive table piled high with mountains of bread. I remarked to a fellow student, "Wow, I didn't realize that our school distributes bread to the needy in the city. That's really great." He gave me a confused look. "Needy? This bread is for us. Seminary is so expensive, many students can't even afford bread!" As he said this a mad-rush of seminarians descended upon the table and began to shove bread into their mouths and backpacks. I remember later that day glancing down at my own financial statements. After twenty good years, my stock had experienced significant growth. Enough growth that I was able to pay for this season of pursuing my dream to study the Word of God. Then it struck me, in this moment, twenty years later, he who once felt less than blessed was singing the praises of City Grandma.

Why am I telling you about this series of events? To illustrate how oftentimes what we want in the moment is not always what is best for us in the long run. And what is best for us, we do not always value and appreciate. Some gifts are more welcomed than others. Why wasn't a seven-year-old thrilled with stock? Ignorance. It took love and wisdom for City Grandma to give me a gift that I was not able to value at the time. Which brings us back to singleness and dating. Sometimes the most loving gift God can give us is singleness.

The Gift of Being Single

Why would I call singleness a gift? Because that is exactly what the apostle Paul called it in 1 Corinthians 7: "I wish that all were as I myself am. But each has his own gift from God, one of one kind and one of another. To the unmarried and the widows I say that it is good for them to remain single, as I am" (vv. 7–8). Don't miss this. Paul just called singleness a gift.[1]

Yet many singles I know long to be connected to somebody. Current surveys of millennials indicate that nearly 96 percent long to be married at some point. So singleness is a gift that the vast majority of us don't want. Some of you may be okay with it now, but as the years go by, this is a gift you might come to resent. "Wow, you got me a present, God? How nice. Wait, singleness? What kind of gift is this? Why would you do this?"

The Reason You Are Single

Why would a loving God give us the gift of singleness when we long to be married? First Corinthians 7:35 gives us the answer. Paul declared, "I say this for your own benefit." Paul had just said that he wished his audience was single. Now he was explaining that this wish was not cruel, but rather for their good. It is a condition that can provide benefit to them. He continued, "Not to lay any restraint upon you." This literally means "not to put a rope around your neck."[2] God's decision to make you single for a season is not to choke you. It is not to hold you back or hurt you. It certainly does not arise from a sick sense of humor in God. He is not laughing maniacally, declaring to the angels, "Watch now as I bring the two of them to the same train station in London, then have one go this way and the

> **Sometimes the most loving gift God can give us is singleness.**

other that way and just miss each other. Haha!" That is not how God works.

So then what is singleness for? Paul declared that it exists "to promote what is appropriate and to secure undistracted devotion to the Lord" (NASB). Do not miss this. Verse 35 just told you the two reasons why God has ordained a season of singleness in your life. Let's take them one at a time.

Promote What Is Appropriate

First, you are single to promote good order (ESV) or to promote what is appropriate (NASB). What does that mean? *Appropriate* means "especially suitable or compatible."[3] An action is deemed appropriate if it fits in a given environment. It is a well-informed, well-played response to a context. Conversely, we deem an action to be inappropriate when it does not fit a given context, like wearing a swimsuit to a wedding. There is nothing wrong with a swimsuit, but it is inappropriate attire for a wedding. Why? It does not fit the context. Context determines the appropriateness of a behavior.

How does this relate to singleness? The Bible declares that God made you single right now because he wants to promote in you a worldview and a lifestyle that fits your environment. You are single because God wants to champion something in you. He wants to foster a way of seeing and a way of living that fits the occasion we live in—that is appropriate for our given context in this day. This brings up the million-dollar question, what is our context? What is our environment?

Timing Is Everything

Paul explained 1 Corinthians 7:29–31: "This is what I mean, brothers: the appointed time has grown very short. From now on, let those who have wives live as though they had none, and those who mourn as though they were not mourning, and those who rejoice as though they were not rejoicing, and those who buy as though they had no goods, and those who deal with the world as though they had no dealings with it. For the present form of this world is passing away." To be clear, however, Paul was not advocating that his audience ditch their spouses and discontinue all purchases. Rather, he was asserting that singleness, dating, and marriage, while important, are not the main story line of your life.

God cares deeply about your love life and your marriage. I would daresay he cares much more about them than even you do. After all, the institution of marriage is his idea! Yet, while important, these issues only take up a sliver of the Bible. A much bigger story has been, and is even now, playing out in the world. What is it? Earlier in 1 Corinthians 6, Paul stated that the world abounds with fornicators, idolaters, thieves, revilers, swindlers, and the like, and none of them will inherit the kingdom of God. Then he confronted his audience (and you and me) by saying, "And such were some of you" (v. 11).

None of us are what we should be. If all of us reading this book gathered in a room and told our stories, our presentations would include tragic, horrible, broken, inexcusable things that have happened to us, and horrible, sad things that have been perpetrated by us. We have all fallen far short of what God intended for us to be. The world is a mess. Yet, the story line of the Bible is that God is on the move; and in the midst of the darkness, God broke in with a new kingdom. Paul continued, "And such were some of you. But you were washed, you were sanctified, you were justified in the name of the Lord Jesus Christ and by the Spirit of our God."

God has established his kingdom through his Son, Jesus

Christ. He is currently populating this kingdom with foolish, weak, despised, broken people. Shame-filled people. Messy people like you and like me. He is calling us out of the darkness we have lived in. He is cleaning us off and setting us apart for himself. Adopting us into his family and inviting us into his mission. This is the great story of the Bible. It is primarily a story not of relationship with a spouse but of relationship with our King!

This brings us back to verse 29 of chapter 7 when Paul said that the time is short. There is not a lot of time left in the world. He said the day is coming when God will stop the clock and history will come to an end. All those who are his, he will call to a side. Those who are not will be cast away from his presence forever. These are the times we live in—the last days where the world is passing away. It is imperative we understand that the amount of time on the clock should affect how we play the game.

Watch the Clock

I remember the first time I played the Madden video game (for the uninitiated, it's an American football game). I competed against my friend who owned the game. I say "competed," but it was really a slaughter. I was getting destroyed. Yet, toward the end of the game, I started to make some progress. I realized that if I kept calling running plays up the middle, I could slowly drive the ball down the field. So I continued to run the same play over and over again, and it was working. I was going to score! Then suddenly, my controls went dead. The game stopped. I looked to my friend for some kind of explanation.

"You're an idiot," he said.

"What? The game stopped working. How does that make me an idiot?"

"The game stopped because time expired. The game is over. You had a chance to score right at the end, but instead of going for the end zone, you just kept calling these ridiculous five-yard running plays," he said.

"I didn't know it was the fourth quarter! I had no idea the game was about to end."

"Exactly. That's what makes you a fool."

Now, all name-calling aside, he had a point. The amount of time on the clock should have affected the way I played. And this was Paul's point to us in 1 Corinthians. Life is short. Not just for us as individuals, but in all of history. Therefore, when we look at men and women in the world, we should be far more concerned about the state of their soul than their relationship status. The amount of time is short, thus God has ordained a period of time where you're not married or dating to help you focus in on what matters most. As Paul told us, "To promote what is appropriate and to secure undistracted devotion to the Lord" (1 Corinthians 7:35 NASB).

Freedom from Distraction

For many of you this raises a natural question: *Can't I be devoted to the Lord while married? Why do I have to be single?* Notice Paul stated that God ordains singleness in order to secure an undistracted devotion to the Lord.

Dating is great. But dating is distracting. Imagine the last time you attended a church gathering. For some of you, while the band led worship, you read the words and sang along. As the Scriptures were read, you listened carefully and pondered their meaning. As the minister preached, you analyzed and applied what was said. Others of you attended the gathering with somebody cute, or sat down by somebody with some potential. And the entire time the worship band played, you were thinking, *I wonder how I look right now? Should I close my eyes in contemplative worship? Raise my arms?*

Sing louder? Softer? What would look cooler? Wait, did our arms just touch? Did they do it on purpose? What could it mean?

As the Scriptures were read, you debated, Should I hold my Bible out for us both to read? What if my arm starts shaking? Would it be weird? Should I lean in? Is that moving too fast? As the pastor prayed, you leaned in to get another whiff of her hair. Or you looked down to see if his shoes were stylish or sensible. And throughout the entire gathering you were thoroughly distracted! That's why the Puritans used to divide their services. The men would sit on one side of the church and the women would sit on the other side. Have you ever tried to listen to the Word of God preached while sitting next to a woman who smells fantastic? It's not easy. So while dating can be fun, it is distracting. Thus God, in his mercy, has given us a gift called singleness. Why? Because he wants our attention. He wants to secure an undistracted devotion to the Lord. Colossians 1:16 explains that we're made "through him and for him." Augustine said, "We are restless until our hearts find their rest in Thee."[4] Time is short. Our relationship with God matters far more than anything else in this life. So God ordains singleness so that we might be able to focus entirely on the One we were made by and for.

Liberty from Anxiety

Yet some of you may say, "Well, Ben, I don't get it. Why do I have to be single to be devoted to God? My wife and I will seek the Lord together! We'll dedicate our firstborn kid to him if he'll show me The One!" Well, let's return to 1 Corinthians 7. Paul said, "I want you to be free from anxieties. The unmarried man is anxious about the things of the Lord, how to please the Lord. But the married man is anxious about worldly things, how to please his wife, and his interests are divided" (vv. 32–34). Paul was advocating singleness because it gives you a liberty from the anxieties and stresses of marriage. The married man is concerned about pleasing his wife and his interests are divided. Now some of you hear that and think, *Please my wife? Ben, that's exactly the kind of distraction I want to be involved in!* Let me tell you something: there are going to be things that make your wife happy that have nothing to do with stuff you enjoy.

For many of you, as soon as dating gets serious, she's going to have some thoughts on your wardrobe choices. For some of you, this will be a welcome improvement. For others, you will suddenly begin to dress far cuter than you ever imagined. Not only that, but now each holiday that rolls around requires immense thought, creativity, and financial investment to find novel ways to tell her she matters to you.

Then when you get engaged, you enter endless days of choosing bedspreads, duvet covers, throw pillows, floral arrangements, serving platters, flatware, cooking supplies, and place settings. And for hours your sweet bride-to-be is going to look at you and ask, "Do you prefer this design or this one? This plate or that plate? This one or that one? This or that?" And you will desperately try to stay focused mentally and emotionally, but a voice inside will be screaming, *I don't care! Someone help me!*

Then when you get married, you will find you must now spend thousands of dollars of your own money on things you never thought about paying for: a new refrigerator, new washer and dryer, couches, love seats, end tables, and a wide variety of cleaning supplies. Then you will discover that when it comes time to pay for health insurance, it is not a game of simple addition. Married couples must pay more. Now it's not 1 + 1 = 2, it's 1 + 1 = 10! You're going to need a second job. Then when you get home from that job, exhausted, you'll hope that you can simply come home, collapse into the couch, and let cable TV wash over you. Think again! She is going to sit down next to you and ask, "How was your day?" And a sweeping "good" is not going to cut it. She's going to want details, details, details, and then she is going to want to share details of her day with you and you are going to have to turn off the television and listen to her while maintaining eye contact and inserting sympathetic affirmations like, "I would also feel upset if she said that to me." And you are going to look up and realize why all the married men you know look so tired. Their financial, emotional, and social responsibilities have increased exponentially. This is why their testosterone levels have hit the floor and their hair is falling out (I'm told). Now none of this is evil, but it is heavy, and it is stressful. It's a lot to manage and it will be distracting.

Ladies, it's the same for you! Paul went on to say, "The unmarried or betrothed woman is anxious about the things of the Lord, how to be holy in body and spirit. But the married woman is anxious about worldly things, how to please her husband" (v. 34). There are going to be all kinds of things that please your husband that are not things you've ever had to think about, worry about, or care about.

There will be things his mama did for him that he's now going to assume you will do, like clean the house or cook breakfast. You're going to think, *Oh, no. We do that together.* He's probably going to be okay with a level of cleanliness that you find completely unacceptable. Go look at a guy's apartment right now. You're going to have to take care of the house and he's just going to want to sit on the couch and play video games.

Which will make you question, "Can we just turn it off for a second to talk about the fact that my parents are coming this weekend? Are we going to make some plans?"

And he'll likely respond, "Oh, it's fine."

Then you'll be like, "Oh my gosh. No, I had something stressful happen today and you're supposed to be my best friend, my soul mate, and process with me."

You'll finally get his attention, and you'll start unpacking a very real and very serious problem and he's just going to kind of stare at you, drooling and blinking.

Which is when you'll think, *I don't think he understands me.*

Let me just tell you now: he doesn't.

Which means you're going to have to figure out how to live with a huge, hairy, confused person.

Then when kids get in the mix you enter a new universe of obligation. Now you have to keep small humans alive! I remember when I was young and single, I decided to go on a weekend retreat with a few married couples from my church. So I stuffed some clothes in a backpack, threw it in the backseat of my truck, and said, "Let's ride." But we didn't leave. For the next several hours I waited as they loaded their minivan with all manner of equipment designed to contain, feed, and entertain their small children. Then we loaded the back of my truck with more equipment. Then we loaded a trailer. It took forever! The entire time the kids were hungry, tired, whiny, and crying. I remember watching my married friends and thinking, *You are encumbered. Everything takes so long!* It hit me in that moment the power available to me in my singleness. I could go to Starbucks right now if I wanted to. I didn't have to ask somebody. I didn't have to make plans. I could just go, spend some money, and drink a latte. At any moment. On a whim. Not so for the married. There are so many hoops to jump through, details to evaluate, people to consider. It's exhausting and time-consuming.

As a husband and a father, I deal with these responsibilities every moment of the day. Recently one of my single staff members asked me if I had seen a particular TV show. I said no. Then she asked about three other shows. I hadn't seen any of those either. She couldn't believe it. How have I not seen any of them? I responded, "I have three children under the age of five. I have thirty minutes of discretionary time each day. That's it." After a stunned moment she replied, "I have about six hours a day." I replied, "Oh, I know. I remember those days, and for me, those days are over."

Now if it sounds like I am down on the institution of marriage, let me assure you I am not. I love being married! I love being a dad! I would not trade the season of life I am in for anything. But I am stressing the encumbrances of marriage in order to save you from a danger that is easy for people in all different stages of life to fall into. There is a tendency in every one of us to downplay the benefits of their stage in life and amplify the benefits of another. The single person pines away for the intimacy of the married season of life. The married man or woman romanticizes the freedoms they enjoyed as a single person. I do not want you to do that. I don't want you to miss out on what you have access to in your single years that you will not have when you're married. I don't want you to miss the benefits of now, because you're fixated on the benefits of then.

The Gift of Freedom

What you have now is freedom and time. These are resources granted to you when you are single that will diminish over time. You have more freedom and more time than any other kind of person on the planet. Children don't have the kind of freedom you do. Old people don't have your level of freedom. Married people don't either. You have an unprecedented amount of discretionary time in this fast-dwindling season that you are in right now. It is freedom with a purpose. Not to fill it with distractions, but to pursue an undistracted devotion to the Lord. That's what it's for. So I want to challenge some of you who are pining away. It is okay to long to be in a relationship and long to be married. That longing is good. The ache for companionship existed in Adam before the entrance of sin in Genesis 3. But if you let that desire steal all the joy of your present single stage, you are missing out on the benefits available to you in this season of life right now. I wholeheartedly agree with the counsel the young missionary Jim Elliot wrote to the young woman he loved while they were oceans apart and not yet married: "Let not our longing slay our appetite for living."[5]

God has ordained the single season for a purpose, and I want you to live it to the hilt. Paul stated in verse 32 of 1 Corinthians 7, "The unmarried man is anxious about the things of the Lord, how to please the Lord." He continued in verse 34, "the unmarried . . . woman is anxious about the things of the Lord, how to be holy in body and spirit." So let me ask you the critical question: Does this define your singleness? As an unmarried man, are you anxious to find ways to please the Lord? As an unmarried woman, are you straining to consider how you might be holy to the Lord in body and spirit? Let me challenge you: if this does not define your singleness, then you are doing singleness wrong.

God has given you singleness to secure an undistracted devotion to the Lord, not to fill your time with distractions. Its purpose is to pursue him. If you are frustrated or bitter in your singleness, it may be because you are missing the point of why you are single. It is like playing basketball without a ball. It is confusing, is frustrating, and, in the end, just feels stupid. Singleness is the same way. If these unmarried moments of your life are not spent in passionate pursuit of your Maker, then they will often be marked by a sense of aimlessness and frustration. Conversely, the most content single people I have ever known are the ones who understood this season is for undistracted devotion to the Lord.

Freedom with Purpose

I entered full-time ministry right out of college. A few years into it, I decided to take an evening seminary class on the life of Christ. A friend of mine who was living and working in downtown Houston decided to join me. During every break between lectures I listened in as my friend was repeatedly asked the following question by different members of the class: "So, what do you do for a living?" He would always give the same reply: "Well, I sell steel to make a living." But then he would always add, "But what I live for is mentoring high school students through Young Life. I absolutely love it."

I remember marveling at my friend. I knew he could have spent every night going out with his friends or watching TV at his house. I am not saying he never did either of those things, but he also decided to carve out time in his schedule every week to invest in the younger generation. Then he dedicated a night every week to study the life of Jesus because he had the time and because he wanted to grow in his knowledge and love for the Lord. That's a good use of singleness.

When I was young and single, I was a youth pastor. One Sunday morning I was sitting in a back hallway of the school we would rent each week to set up our portable church. I was trying to coalesce some thoughts for the sermon I was about to deliver, when one of my young junior high boys walked by.

"Hey, how you doing, man?" I asked him.

"I'm okay," he responded.

But I knew he wasn't. I knew he had gone to stay downtown with his dad because his parents had just split up. His dad was with another lady.

"Yeah, I was helping my dad move in."

"How did that go?"

"It's fine. It's good."

I remember sensing that this was more than just a small-talk moment. This young man was right in the middle of watching the foundations of his family life crumble, and he was trying to tell me what I imagine he was hearing over and over again, that everything was fine. I don't normally speak this way to kids, but in that moment I said to him, "Hey, I know God is going to take care of you and I know you are going to be okay, but this whole situa-

I don't want you to miss the benefits of now because you're fixated on the benefits of then.

tion sucks. And it's okay to say it sucks." He immediately burst out crying and fell into my arms. As a twenty-four-year-old man, I had never experienced something like this before. But then it struck me: *Where else was he going to go?* His dad was no longer a safe person to process these emotions with. Mom wasn't either. His fellow twelve-year-olds didn't have the emotional maturity to help him process all that was happening around him. So this young man had nowhere to go with this pain and he was trying to convince himself, *It's okay*, when it absolutely was not.

I remember sitting there, and I thought about all that it had cost me to be single in the suburbs. All that I didn't have in my life. But I remember sitting in that moment, holding this kid, and I thought, *God, thank you. There is no other place I would rather be than using the time and energy I have now to invest in these kids. Thank you, God, for this moment.* I want that for you. You have more freedom and more time now than you will likely have in the future. I want you to maximize it. You may not be in vocational ministry, but you know the pain and awkwardness of being young. You can invest your time in the next generation. That would be an amazing use of singleness.

Seize the Day

When I visited Venezuela as a single guy in my mid-twenties, we had a young man showing us around who had impeccable English. I asked him, "Where did you learn English? Did you go to school for that? How did you become so proficient at it?" He answered, "I learned it by listening to the radio." I exclaimed, "What?!" He responded, "Yeah. I would just sit and listen to the radio and I taught myself English." I remember thinking, *Now that is a guy who knows how to maximize his time!*

Before Eve came along, Adam named a ton of animals while he was single. You can get a lot done in your singleness. But you must pursue an undistracted devotion to the Lord, not pursue distractions to fill the time. It makes me crazy when I read statistics like those quoted by Philip Zimbardo, chair of the Western Psychological Foundation, in his book *The Demise of Guys*. He reported that the average person, by the time they turn twenty-one, has spent ten thousand hours playing video games. It takes half of that to earn your bachelor's degree.[6] I do not care if you play video games. But if it is a regular part of your life, I wonder if you are missing the bigger story playing out around you? The world around us is on fire today with war, slavery, injustice, and crippling poverty. We need some real heroes to rise up and leverage their gifts for the glory of God and the good of humanity. Please do not spend this season of your life saving fantasy worlds on a screen while the real world is on fire.

The year I got married, a massive tsunami hit the coast of Thailand, killing almost a quarter million people. As I watched the tragedy unfold on the news, I called up a good friend and asked him, "Did you hear about the tsunami?" He said, "Yeah, I'm going." And I replied, "I knew it." I knew it because he was a guy who had flexibility with work, so he thought, *You know what? I'm young and single, and there's a place with a massive humanitarian crisis. I'm going.* I had just gotten married and we didn't have much money, so I couldn't go. I remember admiring his decision and thinking, *That's something his singleness affords him.*

Pursuing Devotion

We have established that singleness offers time to pursue devotion to the Lord. But what does the pursuit of devotion look like? The word *devotion* in Greek is the combination of two concepts— the word *good*, or *well*, and the phrase "to be close beside." It suggests both a passive element of sitting and listening to someone and an active element of tending to his or her desires. A great English word that captures this meaning is the word *attentive*. Think of a good waiter at a restaurant. He is attentive in both of these respects. He is attentive to your words, listening carefully as you speak. He is also attending to your wishes, working hard to fulfill your desires. We are meant to be attentive to the Lord in the same way. Devotion expresses itself in attentiveness to his Word and attending to his work. Study and service. The pursuit of intimacy with him and activity that pleases him.

Attentive to His Word

I had to read a sizable amount of required texts while in college. Consequently, I did not read much in my free time. When I graduated, however, it struck me: *I don't have to read a required book ever again. I can read whatever I want!* In the same moment it occurred to me that though I had been a Christian for many years, I had never read the entire Bible. I believed it was the very words of God, but I hadn't taken the time to read all of them! So I began to take time every morning to slowly read through the entire Bible. I also found that I had ample discretionary time in the evenings after work. I deeply desired to really know God, so I began to ask myself how I could cultivate that intimacy. For me, this line of thinking culminated in getting rid of my TV. For the first few years after college, I would spend several nights a week listening to sermons or slowly copying books of the Bible by hand. I designated an hour one evening a week to go on a walk with God and pray. Sometimes it felt a little like studying for school. Other times the truth would illuminate my mind and warm my heart in such powerful ways that I couldn't wait to tell someone about all that the Lord was teaching me about himself, myself, and the world around me.

Have you set aside regular time to meditate on the Word of God? Take a moment and look over your weekly schedule. Ask God to show you where that time may be. Find a place you like to sit. Develop a plan that gives you a sense of progress each day. Try writing out a book of the Bible. There are 104 verses in the book of Philippians. If you wrote out three verses a day you could hand-write the entire book in just over a month. Give it a shot. Why do this? It makes you move slowly. Take about ten minutes to write out the verses, and then take twenty to thirty more minutes to really meditate upon them. Consider writing the verses in one color and your own thoughts and feelings in a different one. Make it an ongoing dialogue with the Lord.

Attentive to His Work

Devotion to the Lord is cultivated not only in study but also out in the field. We grow in our knowledge and love of God as we engage both his Word and his work. If you were living in the first century and you wanted to walk with Jesus, you would need to search for him among the poor. Jesus traveled among those in need. In the same way today, if you want to be devoted to the Lord, know that he will constantly call you toward those who are spiritually, emotionally, and physically in need.

In 2016 I was the director of Breakaway, a ministry on the campus of Texas A&M. That year we had three young, single people on staff who researched, planned, and executed a fund-raising effort to provide resources to churches in the Middle East who were attempting to provide care for the more than nine million refugees fleeing war-torn Syria. One of the young women on our team tirelessly researched the right organizations, established partnerships, and set goals for our students' involvement. Another staffer organized our media and communications. A single guy on our team created videos that provided perspective to our college students on the refugee crisis. The three of them worked hard to find out where the needs were, articulate them to our college students, and then put together an organized method of collecting funds. The result: in a little more than a month, they raised more than a quarter million dollars. What a tremendous way to spend their singleness! Whatever happens next in their lives, they will be able to say, "I worked hard to alleviate human suffering in the world." I want that to be true of you as well. Get involved in your local church. Discover more about their local and global efforts to relieve suffering in the name of Jesus. Then join in the work! I promise there is deep satisfaction when you realize that the work of your hands today can have a substantial impact in the lives of people in your city and around the world.

Is Singleness More Spiritual?

Before we close this chapter, I want to answer one final question some of you may be asking. Namely, is singleness more spiritual?

Paul stated in 1 Corinthians 7:8–9, "To the unmarried and the widows I say that it is good for them to remain single, as I am. But if they cannot exercise self-control, they should marry. For it is better to marry than to burn with passion." Now some of you hear that and you think, *If it's more spiritual to be single, I don't care. I fit squarely into the burning with passion category. I'm on fire, so bring on the spouse!* Yet others of you hear this admonition and think, *I really want to serve the Lord, and if it's more spiritual to stay single the rest of my life, then I want to be open to that.* So we must answer this critical question: Is it more spiritual to be single than to be married?

Let me address this question with a passage where Jesus spoke on the subject of singleness. Specifically, he addressed the plight of eunuchs. Without going into a great deal about what makes one a eunuch (feel free to ask your pastor), let's just say they are those who are unable to have children. Addressing his disciples in Matthew 19:12, Jesus said, "For there are eunuchs who have been so from birth, and there are eunuchs who have been made eunuchs by men." (That's the most unfortunate group in this whole passage.) "And there are eunuchs who have made themselves eunuchs for the sake of the kingdom of heaven. Let the one who is able to receive this receive it."

For our purposes, let's focus on the final group. Jesus identified that there are some who have chosen singleness for the sake of advancing the purposes of God. They have foregone marriage and children in order to devote more time and energy into advancing the purposes of God on earth. Some of you hear this and ask, "Is that supposed to be me? Am I supposed to do that? How will I know? I want to be married, but I also very much want to serve the Lord. Will those always be at odds?"

Our answer comes one verse earlier: "He said to them, 'Not everyone can receive this saying, but only those to whom it is given.'" Some of you have been given singleness for a season, and, in due time, this season will pass. Sooner, for some of you, a little later for others. For some of you it will tarry for a while, but the God who has given you the gift of singleness will give you the grace to endure it. But some of you will be like Augustine or Origen, or Amy Carmichael, Mother Teresa, or the apostle Paul, or Jesus, and live your life unmarried. Let me encourage you: an unmarried life is not an unfulfilled life. You can have deep fulfillment and be unmarried. Others of you will be like the apostle Peter, or Jesus' brothers, or me. God will give you somebody to marry, and you will get to live life with that person and it will be a great gift. The married apostle Peter and the single apostle Paul linked arms and made a difference for the kingdom, and, by the grace of God, we are meant to do the same.

But whether your season of singleness is long or short, you can know that God has granted you this season as a gift, and it is a gift with a purpose: to pursue an undistracted devotion to him. All that is left is for you to ponder the question: *What will that look like for me?*

3

a singleness case study

the apostle paul // 2 timothy 4:9–22

Someone to Chase

While I was a student at Texas A&M University I ran a marathon. As I trained I discovered that it really is true: when you get out there on long runs your body's chemicals get a little crazy and you can get on an emotional roller coaster. There really is a runner's high and it feels amazing. But you can also hit some emotional lows. On one particular long run during training, I hit a major low, and it was painful. In the space of a mile I went from a run . . . to a walk . . . to a hobble. Then it started to rain. Everything in me wanted to just quit and do something easier, like sit. But I was miles from home, so I had no choice but to keep going. I realized I needed to think of something to motivate me. The image that came to mind was of Chris, my Bible study leader. He had run the Houston Marathon the year the city had frozen over. It was so cold ice had formed on runners' hats while they ran! I remember standing at the finish line and watching runner after runner collapse with leg cramps or in sheer exhaustion. Yet, there, amid the chaos, came Chris charging toward the line, finishing strong. As I replayed this memory in my mind, it stirred something deep within me. I wanted to finish well too. I wanted to rise up strong and be victorious in life. There in my emotionally volatile state I began to tear up as I said, at first to myself, then out loud, "I want to be like Chris." The

> **Leverage this season for the glory of God.**

more I thought about this beautiful reality, the less I thought about my pain. I stood back up. "I want to be like Chris." I began to jog again. As I continued to contemplate the heroic act of my mentor, I began to break into a sprint. By the end of my run I am sure that anyone who saw me thought I was nuts. I charged through campus at a dead sprint, tears streaming down my face, screaming, "I WANT TO BE LIKE CHRIS!"

Why tell you this?

What I needed in my moment of struggle was someone before me whose life could inspire and instruct me to run my race well. We all need this in life as well. As we talk about singleness and how to leverage this season for the glory of God, we need a picture of someone who did that well. The apostle Paul can be that inspiration for us. He told the Philippians to, "Follow me as I follow Christ" (1 Corinthians 11:1 MEV).

So in this case study I want to set Paul's life before us so that it might inspire and instruct us as we consider maximizing our singleness. In order to do this, I want to walk you through the last words of the apostle Paul, written to his young protégé Timothy. At the end of his life, Paul was imprisoned in Rome for preaching the gospel. From his cell he wrote to Timothy, his beloved disciple, who was probably in his twenties at the time. To the Corinthians Paul referred to him as "my beloved and faithful son" (1 Corinthians 4:17 NKJV). Paul told the Philippians, "I have no one else like him" (Philippians 2:20 NIV). The Christian life brings with it deep relationships. And here at the end, as Paul sat in prison anticipating his death, his thoughts turned to his dear son in the faith. In the last few lines in his letter, we get a window into what the end of a single life lived well looks like.

When I was young and single, I listened to the pastor of Denton Bible Church, Tommy Nelson, teach on 2 Timothy 4:9–22. Tommy's words, which significantly informed this chapter, changed the trajectory of my single years and continue to shape my life today. I hope these next few pages will supply you with a vision of what your single years can be. Before we get started, please take a few minutes to read 2 Timothy 4:9–22. Then, we will review eight things that are true of Paul as he crossed the finish line of life. Lord willing, may these things be true of us as well.

1. Resolve to Never Stop

In 2 Timothy 4:10–12 we see our first point of how to maximize your singleness. Paul wrote, "Crescens has gone to Galatia, Titus to Dalmatia. . . . Pick up Mark . . . he is useful to me for service. But Tychicus I have sent to Ephesus" (NASB). Do you see what was happening? Even from a prison cell at the end of his life Paul was coordinating a ministry that was operating on five fronts. Nothing could stop Paul from his mission of making Christ's name known, not even imprisonment or impending death! That is meant to be our attitude.

Make the decision now that nothing in life will keep you from fulfilling the purposes of your great King. Never quit. Paul wanted death to be his finish line. You should too.

You may retire from your profession, but you never retire from your mission. Not until the Lord calls us off the field. This mind-set will keep you from letting any discouragement derail you, any busyness from swallowing up your time, or any secondary issue from taking your primary energy. Paul did not sit and cry in his cell. He didn't allow his circumstances to become excuses. Instead, he turned his prison into a mission-control center for gospel expansion! Discouragements and distractions will abound in your life, but the people who make the greatest impact in the world are those who resolve early that, no matter what comes, they will never quit.

2. Invest in the Next Generation

And look how Paul conducted his ministry: through investment in the next generation. Paul, at the end of his life, was surrounded by young men whom he had mentored. I want that, too, don't you? I implore you: regardless of your age, in your pursuit of God, do not neglect the great work of imparting the truths of God to the next generation. Jesus made this a priority in his ministry from the very start, selecting those who might "be with him and he might send them out to preach" (Mark 3:14). If we want to live a life of impact, then we cannot be indifferent about our personal investment in the lives of people. The future of the church depends on it.

There is an old African proverb that says, "If we do not initiate the boys, they will burn the village down."[1] At the time of this writing more than 40 percent of the children born in the United States do not have a father in the home. One-third of all boys in the United States are growing up in fatherless homes.[2] More than 40 percent of teens report that they have dinner with their family less than five times per week, which, according to the National Center on Addiction and Substance Abuse, makes them twice as likely to use alcohol and four times more likely to use drugs.[3] When Paul met Timothy he was a young man with an absent father. By this time Timothy was now the pastor of one of the most influential churches in the world. Without Paul's investment would Timothy have been able to reach that potential? Players need coaches. Young men and women need mentors.

In ancient Rome baby girls were often seen as an absorption of wealth. So if a baby girl was born and the family did not want her, they could lay the baby out on the side of the road. There she would either die of exposure or be picked up by a pimp and used in a brothel. Early Christians abhorred this act of infanticide because they believed those little girls had dignity as they, too, were made in the image of God. But rather than simply wag their fingers or shake their heads at corrupt Rome, they made a decision. If our culture will not raise these girls, we will. If you were to stop by the worship gathering of our earliest brothers and sisters in the faith, you would be greeted by the singing voices of little girls, praising a God who comes to get us when we are at our lowest.

Let me challenge you: When you think about your plans for the future, do they include the men and women you will invest in? Paul commanded Timothy to entrust the truths of God in reliable men who will be able to teach others (2 Timothy 2:2). He commanded women to train up younger women (Titus 2:3–4). In Psalm 71, as the psalmist contemplated the end of his life he uttered a simple prayer, "When I am old and gray, O God, do not forsake me, until I declare Your strength to this generation, Your power to all who are to come" (v. 18 NASB). I promise you, you will find deep satisfaction in this work during your single years. In 3 John 4, the apostle declared, "I have no greater joy than to hear that my children are walking in the truth." You want joy like that? Invest in the next generation.

3. Cultivate Deep Friendships

Not only was Paul surrounded by protégés, he also had good friends. He said in 2 Timothy 4:11, "Only Luke is with me" (NASB). This is our third point: cultivate deep friendships. I use the word *cultivate* because it is a gardening image, and gardening takes time. You can't rush the gardening process. If you want to see a substantive and fruitful tree grow, you will need to intentionally invest energy over time. Most of us have acquaintances and coworkers. We have the people we hang with. But this is more than that. Proverbs 18:24 states, "A man of many companions may come to ruin, but there is a friend who sticks closer than a brother." For Paul, that was Luke. As Paul's journeys are recounted throughout the book of Acts (which Luke wrote), the pronouns switch from "they" to "we." Luke was personally there for much of the ride. And here at the end, Luke was still with him. As a physician, he was probably keeping Paul's beaten-up body alive! Do you have a friend like that? Someone who will walk through the fire with you? Someone who will keep you alive emotionally, or even physically, in the tough times?

Our normal rhythms of life in this culture promote shallowness. Loneliness and isolation are always creeping at the door, and we must battle them. Not necessarily with a broad swath of thousands of friends, but with a few, close, deep friendships.

I hate to say this, but nearly every year I see men fall out of ministry or lose their families because of some epic scandal in their life. Though their particular brands of sin may change, one common denominator is true in all of them: they neglected the work of developing close friendships. So when the struggles came, they were battling their external stresses and inner turmoil alone. In your season of singleness, and even in married life, you can stand strong in the stresses and strains in life if you prioritize developing relationships with those who love God, love you, and aren't afraid to tell you when you're being an idiot. King Solomon lamented, "Pity anyone who falls and has no one to help them up" (Ecclesiastes 4:10 NIV). You don't want to be that guy or girl. Cultivate deep friendships.

4. Keep Learning

As we move into 2 Timothy 4:13, Paul made a surprising request: "When you come bring the cloak which I left at Troas with Carpus, and the books, especially the parchments" (NASB). Parchment was expensive, so these probably contained more valued writings. Though we cannot be sure, some scholars speculate this may have been Paul's copy of the Scriptures. Whatever books they may have been, it is fascinating to note that even while in prison, Paul wanted to keep reading. Paul, the prolific writer, even after all he had preached and accomplished, wanted to keep learning. This is a great way to spend your singleness: keep learning.

When the reformer Martin Luther was in danger of assassination, his supporters had him sequestered in Wartburg Castle from 1521 to 1522. Desiring to maximize his time, Luther used that season to translate the entire New Testament from the original Koine Greek texts into contemporary German. In doing so he made the Word of God accessible to the people of his nation in a way they had never experienced before. You may not use your spare time for Bible translation, but you can certainly set aside time to keep growing in knowledge.

In his book *When I Don't Desire God*, John Piper explained that if you read two hundred words per minute (about the speed you can read audibly at a natural pace) for fifteen minutes a day, then you can easily read ten substantive books each year.[4] In 2014 the average American spent forty minutes a day on Facebook alone.[5] Redirect a third of that time each day toward reading and you will get a whole lot smarter. Aim some of that time at Bible study and you will gain a lot more than just intelligence. The psalmist declared in Psalm 1 that those who meditate on the Word of God are "like a tree planted by streams of water that yields its fruit in its season, and its leaf does not wither. In all that he does, he prospers" (v. 3). Do you want to be productive in the good times and persevering in the bad? Then keep learning.

5. Make Enemies

The next way to maximize your singleness may surprise you. In verses 14–15 of 2 Timothy 4 Paul warned Timothy: "Alexander the coppersmith did me much harm; the Lord will repay him according to his deeds. Be on guard against him yourself, for he vigorously opposed our teaching" (NASB).

Notice the nature of Paul and Alexander's disagreement. It was not a personality conflict. It was a strong opposition to Paul's teaching! Alexander knew what Paul believed about Jesus. He understood that Paul believed that we are all dead because of our sin, but can have life eternal in Jesus Christ. Alexander hated that message. Therefore, he hated Paul.

This is meant to be true of all people who follow Christ. Jesus himself warned us in Luke 6:26, "Woe to you when all men speak well of you, for their fathers used to treat the false prophets in the same way" (NASB). Does everybody like you? That may be a problem. Now let me be clear: the goal is not to proactively make enemies. The goal is to stand for something. When you are really leveraging your life for something that matters, you will face resistance. Eleven of the twelve disciples faced violent deaths. If no one ever resists you, it may be because you are not a voice of positive change in your culture. To change the world, we must speak the truth. To speak the truth will invite criticism. Don't be discouraged. That resistance may be a sign that you are on the right track.

6. Forgive

Notice how Paul handled the hate. He told Timothy, "The Lord will repay him according to his deeds" (2 Timothy 4:14). There was no urging Timothy to try to get even with Alexander for Paul's sake. There was no attempt on Paul's part to call down curses on this man's head. Rather, Paul obeyed his own injunction in Romans

12, reminding himself that the Lord has said, "Vengeance is mine, I will repay" (v. 19).

And it is not only this enemy that Paul forgave, but also his friends! A few verses later Paul explained, "At my first defense no one supported me, but all deserted me" (2 Timothy 4:16 NASB). The "first defense" was most likely Paul's initial hearing before the courts in Rome concerning his current imprisonment. During those trials it was common for supporters to come forward and appeal for mercy or give a defense for the accused. What happened at Paul's first defense? No one showed up to support him. There were Christians in Rome. Paul mentioned some in the shout-out section of the letter a few verses later. But as his charges were read, he stood alone. That had to have hurt. Yet, again, notice his attitude. Paul declared, "May it not be counted against them" (v. 16 NASB). He refused to nurse bitterness. Rather, like Jesus on the cross, he "entrust[ed] himself to him who judges justly" (1 Peter 2:23). We must learn to forgive like this.

> **Paul maximized his view of God.**

Like Paul, many of us have been deeply wounded. Maybe it was a cruel employer or a kid at school. Maybe it was by an authority figure or family member who should have been a source of safety. I do not know what you have been through, but I know that all of us have been hurt at some point or another. I also know that we must learn to forgive. If not, the resentment we feel toward that person will not stay in that one compartment of our heart. Once we light the fire of unforgiveness in our heart, then decide to stoke the flames of bitterness and resentment, we do not get to be master of that flame. Fire doesn't work that way. It will burn your house down. Corrie ten Boom, a Christian watchmaker who was imprisoned by the Nazis during World War II because she helped many Jews escape the Holocaust, said the following:

Since the end of the war I had had a home in Holland for victims of Nazi brutality. Those who were able to forgive their former enemies were able also to return to the outside world and rebuilt their lives, no matter what the physical scars. Those who nursed their bitterness remained invalids. It was as simple and as horrible as that.[6]

How do we forgive like that? Notice Paul did not minimize the wrongs done to him. He acknowledged that they were hurtful actions. Rather, Paul maximized his view of God in the moment. The Lord will repay Alex. The Lord will forgive the fearful saints. Paul saw that, at the end of the day, God controlled the narrative of his life, not the perpetrators of wrongdoing.

Many of you will get married in the years ahead. I promise you, it will only help the future health of your marriage if you go through whatever journey you must now to forgive those who have hurt you in your past. If you refuse to forgive the strangers or family members who have hurt you in the past, how will you forgive your spouse in the future, who is sure to wound you? Get the counseling and support you need as a single person to work through issues of forgiveness now. Resting in the sovereign care of God will empower forgiveness of your enemies. And forgiveness will cultivate in your soul a sweetness that will serve you well in every relationship you have in the future.

7. Be Courageous

Verse 16 paints a sad picture: Paul stood alone as he faced condemnation. But then in 2 Timothy 4:17 he declared, "But the Lord stood with me and strengthened me, so that through me the proclamation might be fully accomplished, and that all the Gentiles might hear; and I was rescued out of the lion's mouth" (NASB).

Paul looked to his right and left and found no person by his side. But he was not alone. The Lord stood with him. Not only did he draw comfort from this, but it filled him with sufficient courage to proclaim the gospel, even in the midst of his trial. Paul had been told when he became a Christian that he would one day proclaim Jesus to kings. I am sure he did not imagine he would do it in chains. Nevertheless, he saw this moment as an opportunity and he took it, knowing that it might get him killed. Yet Paul was willing to take the risk so that all the nations might know the hope available in Christ. That is a powerful way to spend your singleness!

I am not encouraging you at this moment to court death, but I know many of us often find ourselves in situations where an allegiance to Christ may cost us socially, professionally, financially, or physically. Yet Paul did it, not to prove he wasn't scared or to earn God's approval. Instead, he did it for the sake of those who might believe through him. I want to challenge you: leverage your circumstances for the advance of the gospel. Paul did not seek to be put in prison, but he used prison as a platform for evangelism.

I don't know what school, job, city, or social sphere God has placed you in. But I challenge you to begin to pray that the Lord might show you how to leverage that situation for gospel expansion. As a young man, Jim Elliot wrote in his journal, "Father, make of me a crisis man. Bring those I contact to decision. Let me not be a milepost on a single road; make me a fork, that men must turn one way or another on facing Christ in me."[7]

8. Rest

The Lord will rescue me from every evil deed, and will bring me safely to His heavenly kingdom; to Him be the glory forever and ever. Amen. (2 Timothy 4:18 NASB)

Finally, Paul rested in the care of God.

I marvel at Paul's sign-off when I contemplate what a letter from prison written by me might sound like. Mine would likely include something like, "HELP! Get me out of here! There's been a mistake! I want to go home!" This type of response would be completely consistent with someone who was only viewing his or her immediate physical situation. But Paul had a broader view. He entrusted his enemies to the sovereign justice of God. He entrusted his wavering friends to the mercy of God. Now he trusted all of his life to the hands of God. The Lord saved me at my trial. The Lord will care for me going forward. And when I do die, the Lord will take me home.

Paul did not see himself as a hero or a warrior. He saw himself like a child or a little sheep. I do not control my circumstances, but I am held by the One who can cradle the seas in the hollow of his hand. I'm going to be fine. Paul died pointing toward the heavens—to him be the glory forever and ever! This is a great way to live life and a great way to sign off. I control so little of what happens in life, but I am known and loved by the Author of life.

If this is your perspective, then you can have peace. You can trust God with your longings for marriage, knowing he hears you and cares. You can trust him with your career plans, because you know he determines your steps. You can trust him with your inevitable decline in health, because you know that if you are in Christ death is not the end for you.

He will carry you safely home. The world marvels at men and women who can exude a confidence like this. People long for a peace like this that surpasses understanding.

This is available to all who trust in the Lord. Each day as you walk through your season of singleness, continue to trust your heart, mind, relationships, plans, and circumstances to the Lord. Commit your way to him, then rest in the arms of a strong and loving Father. I can promise you this is the most fruitful and peaceful way to live your life until he calls you home.

dating: evaluation

Dating is not a status to dwell in, but a process to move through. It is a series of actions meant to lead us to a particular end—discerning whether or not we are meant to marry a particular person. Dating exists for evaluation.

4

who to date

During Spring Break of my freshman year of college, I remember standing on the beach on Padre Island, declaring my affections to my on-again-off-again girlfriend and telling her I wanted to date. We then hopped into a horse-drawn carriage to take a romantic ride down the moonlit beach. As we prepared to embark, to my surprise, we were joined by another guy who, I learned while on the ride, had been interested in her as well. Then we went on a romantic horse-drawn ride—me, her, and this other guy. As we trotted along together, she proceeded to tell me about this dinner he had prepared for her and how it was "the most romantic thing anyone had ever done for her." Riveting story. Just then, the horse ran over some driftwood, shattering the axle on the carriage. As we all went crashing down, I thought, *This feels like a good time for me to exit this scene.* As I walked along the beach alone, I thought, *You know, this might be a good time to exit the idea of dating altogether.*

Yet, I didn't. In fact, my dating exploits over the next few years would become an endless source of comedy for my closest friends. My sophomore year I had to have a tearful breakup with a girl I had never technically dated. The following year, on the same night, another girl and I broke up and had our first kiss—in that order. You may say, "Ben, that doesn't make any sense." I would reply, "I know." So I took a hiatus from dating for about six years. I just couldn't do it without the whole thing ending in a Dumpster fire of confusion, miscommunication, tears, and heartache. Why tell you this? As we enter this section on dating, I want you to know that I have felt the pain. Dating was rough for me before I eventually met Donna.

Dating is tough because it is risky. You can get hurt. There is a reason that Adele and Taylor Swift are both millionaires, and it is not just because they have lights-out amazing voices. Those ladies sing about heartache and the world sings along! Though we can't all monetize our pain the way they have, we can sure belt out our laments along with them.

So if dating can feel like playing hopscotch in a minefield, why risk the inevitable pain? Because deep in us we long to connect. We want to love and we want to be loved. Regardless of the difficulties and dangers of dating, the facts remain that most people on the planet want to get married. So we are willing to risk the drama of dating for the payoff of a long-term, intimate relationship.

In this section, will we talk about how to get a date? Not really. Because here is the reality: anyone can get a date. Anyone can get married. If you set your standards low enough you can get married tonight! Finding someone is easy, but finding the RIGHT someone the RIGHT way is not.

The question then becomes: How do we achieve that? How can we date in a way that will maximize the good aspects of meeting people and minimize the pain? To answer that question, we need to back up and ask something even more fundamental: What is dating for?

I would submit to you that dating is our modern process of

evaluation. What are you evaluating? Another person. What are you looking to discern? Whether or not you want to spend the rest of your life with this person!

Before we dive in, some of you may say, "But aren't you trying to use the Bible as a guide? Ben, the Bible doesn't say a thing about dating." This is true. But it does have much to say to us about *evaluation*. Proverbs 25:24 states, "It is better to live in a corner of the roof than in a house shared with a contentious woman" (NASB). Do you think that was written for the married guy? Some poor dude hanging off the side of his house reading this thinking, *Now you tell me!?* No! It's for the single man evaluating what kind of woman he should marry *before* deciding to marry. Is the girl you are interested in combative? Is she constantly arguing with her roommates? Then you should be careful. If you marry her there will be very little peace in your home. Conversely, you can read a number of verses in the Bible about what an honorable woman looks like. There is a lot in there about the kind of woman who is a gift from God and worth more than fine jewels. Ladies, Proverbs 25:28 warns, "A man without self-control is like a city broken into and left without walls." Does that cute guy have a temper? Does he explode in anger or bully or berate his friends? Don't marry that guy. He won't build up your house. He will destroy it. You will not feel safe living with him. We could keep going, but the point here is that the Scriptures are full of passages like this. So, no, you won't find any Bible verses about dating per se. But the Word of God has much to say about evaluation.

Evaluation leads naturally to two critical questions. The first: What qualities should I look for? This is the *who* question. *Who* should I date and ultimately marry? The second natural question that arises: What process should I go through to find that right person? This is the *how* question. *How* can I date successfully? A great dating experience and, more importantly, a great marriage—one that will last and that you will rejoice over and not regret—is based on these two critical factors: *who* you date and *how* you date. The person and the process. These are the two questions we will seek to answer in this section—who is the right person and what is the right process to go through to get to that person? In this chapter we will look at who to date. In the following chapter we will examine how.

Run Your Race

Picture your life as a race you are running. As a single person, you are charging toward the Lord. Devoted to him. Using your gifts, abilities, time, and influence to be a blessing to all people who are made in his image. As you are chasing after him, there will be all manner of people running as well, but in all manner of directions. Some will cross your path right in front of you. They may even be cute! But they are running in a totally different direction, pursuing things other than God. Maybe they're pursuing money, happiness, fame, or acceptance. In which case you tell yourself, *Hey, they're cute, but I'm not going to try to grab hold of them. Their life is going one way and mine is going another. That's not a good combination.* This kind of evaluation means you are going to let a lot of cute, witty, charming people run right by you, because they are not pursuing the things of God!

But when you are chasing the Lord, after a while you will look up and see people chasing him along with you. As you are running along with those people, you're going to start talking to a few of them. You're going to check them out. And it is okay to start running alongside one of them and see if you two have some chemistry. *Do I like talking to you? Are you fun to be with?* As this happens, you eventually find someone to run with for the rest of your life.

What we are looking for is *character* and *chemistry*. You want someone with character. Not someone who simply acquiesces to the existence of a deity, but someone who passionately pursues God and the things of God. You want to be with a man or woman who possesses a deep, God-shaped character. Then you want to look for someone with whom you have chemistry. Someone you enjoy hanging out with. Someone you enjoy talking to. Someone with whom you click.

Character and chemistry. You must have both. Some people only want chemistry. They meet someone they think is cute, is funny, and with whom they can talk for hours. But they bypass deep conversations about core values. Then they get married. That hot, fun, cool, cute couple gets together and then five, six, or seven years later, when they start to make big life decisions, they realize they have a very different set of values. Those marriages struggle and often come apart. Or, on the other end of the spectrum, you can find someone who has a deep, stalwart character but he or she is so boring that after five minutes you run out of things to say. You do not have to do this to yourself. You need both. You want solid, godly character and fun, easy chemistry.

What you should *not* be looking for is someone to complete you. Dating is not about chasing a person in whose eyes we can find a sense of meaning and fulfillment. That is far too much weight to put on another human being. And that is not how we are built. You are not half of a person waiting for another half of a person to complete you. Jesus and the apostle Paul were

> **You want solid, godly character and fun, easy chemistry.**

not incomplete as singles, and neither are you. No human being will meet every need, solve every problem, heal every wound, or eradicate every insecurity. Those who put pressure on a friendship or a romantic relationship to provide that will always end up crushing the relationship. A relationship is not meant to carry that weight. But you can find someone who has great character and with whom you have great chemistry. Then you can run into the future God has for you together, and that is a pretty amazing ride. That is the vision we are aiming for in marriage: a couple hand in hand, pursuing God together—same direction, same pace, good chemistry. This is what marriage is meant to be. Dating is the modern process of evaluation we use to find that person to marry.

This is no small shift in mind-set. One of the great dangers in modern dating is the tendency to adopt a *consumer* mentality rather than a *companion* mentality.

What I mean by this is that often when you ask someone what kind of person they'd like to date or marry, they begin to list a set of characteristics. "I want him to be tall, but not too tall. Handsome. Funny. Charming. Great job. Solid income. Sensitive but strong. Confident but also caring. And he should have six-pack abs." Or, "I want her to be shorter than me with these specific measurements. She needs to know how to have a good time. She needs to be into sports, running, hiking, travel, saving money, and me." But this mentality causes problems from the start.

Do you hear what is happening when you do this? You are trying to customize your order to get what you think is best for you. This is exactly how you order a burger or curate your playlist. But this is not how you date. Why? Because we are looking for a *person* to love, not a *product* to consume. You are not constructing a robot from human parts. That is not honoring the image of God in the other. We all come as fully functioning human beings.

You cannot assemble one to meet your preferences. That would not be good for you anyway. You would still be a selfish person if you tried to do this. When you date another human, as you grow together you will encourage, challenge, and shape each other. You will have to adapt, change, and sacrifice during this process. The proper question should be, *Could I build a life with this person? Could we journey down the road of life together?* It may seem like a subtle shift in evaluative method, but I promise you being slightly off angle in the wrong direction at the beginning of your evaluation will put you in a very different place in ten years. The problem with a consumer mentality—looking for a person to complete you rather than a companion to run with—is that it creates a perfect recipe for disappointment and discouragement down the road. It does so in four ways.

1. Unrealistic Expectations

First, a consumer mentality creates an expectation that no person can live up to. When we mentally fashion an ideal mate for ourselves, we typically do not select which flaws we would like them to have too. But every person has them. If you take attributes that you like from a variety of sources, and mentally assemble them all into an ideal date, you will not come up with an actual person. And if you then compare real people to this imaginary standard, everyone will disappoint you. But the problem is not with them! You have created a standard that no human being can live up to—even the ones you drew inspiration from. Men imagine marrying a woman who looks like the ones he sees in magazines or online. But those images have been photoshopped. They are not real. The actual women in those images don't look like that in real life. That is why so many girls like magazines like *Us Weekly* and others filled with paparazzi pictures, because they show celebrities in candid moments when they do not look as perfect. It comforts girls who are often all too aware of their shortcomings physically. Ladies will often dream of finding men who are like those they see in romantic movies. But no guys are like that! The actors who play those romantic characters are not even like that. So if you would not like someone to hold you to an impossible standard, then you must not do it to somebody else either. It is a recipe for disappointment. Assembling a checklist of characteristics for a potential mate creates an unfair standard for that person.

2. You Don't Know What You Don't Know

The second reason why we need to abandon a consumer mentality is that it works off the faulty assumption that we actually know what we want. In Dan Slater's history of online dating, entitled *Love in the Time of Algorithms*, he noted that the first online dating services attempted to match clients based on what they said they wanted. A man would type what he wanted—a tall, blonde, educated woman—and then the dating service would attempt to find a person who matched his requests. The only problem was they were not finding much success. People who were a "perfect match" rarely made it past the first date. So in 2008, Match.com hired Amarnath Thombre to track down the flaw in the algorithm. He discovered that the problem was not in the technology, but in the people. He compared what people said they wanted (age, hair color, etc.) with whom they actually contacted to go on a date. What he discovered was there was absolutely no correlation between what people said they wanted and the person whom they ended up with.

"When you watch their browsing habits," he explained, "their actual behavior on the site—you see them go way outside what they say they want."[1] I saw this same tendency with my buddies in college. Many guys would describe the kind of woman they wanted to marry. My close friend told us all that he wanted to marry a wild, adventurous girl who was covered with tattoos. He ended up marrying a sweet, introverted girl who had no tattoos and had never kissed someone. I ended up marrying a wild girl with tattoos!

Who people think they want is often not at all who they actually want. Typically, I have found that peoples' descriptions of their ideal date's attributes are really just idealized versions of themselves. But you don't want to date you, or an ideal version of you. You want to date, and marry, someone who complements you. And believe it or not, the data suggests that you really don't know a lot about what that person will be like.

3. Basing the Permanent on the Transient

The third reason why a consumer mentality fails us in the realm of dating is because it roots our selection process in the most transient of characteristics. You see this most acutely in online dating. As companies discovered that attempts to match based on complex lists of traits were ultimately fruitless, they simplified the programs. Now the most popular dating apps typically give someone two data points about themselves to offer to the world: (1) a picture, and (2) a short witty comment. Looks and charm become the basis for potential lifelong partner selection. But these are the most unreliable characteristics! Proverbs 31:30 warns us, "Charm is deceitful, and beauty is vain, but a woman who fears the LORD is to be praised." Charm is deceitful! Anybody can be charming for an hour over dinner. Charm is easy. Character is harder to fake over time. And beauty is vain. That means it is transient. It goes away. Looks are guaranteed to fade. Plus, you would not want someone to marry you based on these characteristics. Why? Because what if you damaged your face? What if you get injured, as I did, and can't exercise for a few years? What if you get sick and life gets hard and it's not easy to laugh for a good stretch of time? If your marriage is built on surface characteristics, then you have no hope of a lasting future.

4. Dehumanization

The final reason a consumer mentality is a bad approach to dating is because it dehumanizes people. Sheena Iyengar, a Colombia University professor who specializes in choice, said, "People are not products. But essentially, when you say, 'I want a guy that's six foot tall, and has blah, blah, blah characteristics, you're treating a human being like one.'"[2] Jonathan Grant's book *Divine Sex* explains,

In 2011, a consultant to online-dating companies published the results from a survey of thirty-nine of the industry's executives called "How Has Internet Dating Changed Society?" These insiders agreed that online dating had "made people more disposable" and may be partly responsible for a rise in divorce rates.[3]

You can begin to see someone as a product to be used by you instead of a person to be loved by you. Here is the most sinister part. It not only dehumanizes them, but ultimately it dehumanizes *you*. Rather than love people, you want to use people. You were made for more than that. When we know God, we are meant to be a conduit of his grace to others. We leverage our lives to build other people up for the glory of God. We do not leverage other people's lives to further ourselves. That is no subtle difference.

Character: What You Should Be Looking For

We are not looking primarily for a collection of characteristics, but rather for character and chemistry. We are looking for a person who has character before God and chemistry with us. Let's start with exploring three critical factors of character, and what it should look like.

Same Allegiance

This is absolutely critical. You must be aligned on the most important thing in life. Why is this so important? Because your allegiance determines your direction. Different allegiances equate to different directions. It's that simple. A. W. Tozer wrote in his seminal work *The Knowledge of the Holy*, that the most important thing about a person is what he or she thinks about God.[4] I used to wonder what exactly that meant. Now I understand that who you think runs the universe will inform your values. Your values will shape your goals. Your goals will determine where you go in life. So yes, what you believe about who made this place will determine everything you think is important and all that you do. Your allegiance determines your direction. Your mission in life determines a million little decisions you make every single day. So when you are talking about the person you will live the rest of your life with, you want to be lockstep on the biggest issues in life.

Imagine being handcuffed to someone while standing in the middle of Texas. If he wants to walk to LA and you want to walk to Florida, you're going to have a problem. (Beyond the obvious problem of how on earth did you manage to end up handcuffed to someone in the middle of Texas!) How is this going to end up? At some point maybe one of you is strong enough to drag the other, but you aren't going to move very efficiently. You aren't going to have much fun either. It isn't fun to drag someone, and it isn't fun being dragged. Or maybe you both continue to stubbornly fight to go your own way—one east, the other west, and you both end up frustrated, angry, and hurt because you aren't making any progress in life.

This is why Paul warned the followers of Jesus in 2 Corinthians 6:14: "Do not be unequally yoked with unbelievers." What did Paul mean by "unequally yoked"? Paul was referencing Deuteronomy 22:10, a verse addressing issues in farming. A *yoke* was an instrument used to bind animals together while they were plowing a field. You have probably seen them in old photographs. A wooden bar lays across the neck of both animals as they travel side-by-side, pulling a cart or plow. In this passage of Deuteronomy, Moses instructed his people to avoid harnessing together two different types of animals. Why wouldn't you connect an ox and a donkey? Because they are entirely different animals with different wiring and different paces. They will not work well if they are bound together. You will never get where you want to go. Paul took this idea and applied it to human relationships. Those who have sworn allegiance to Jesus Christ should not bind their lives together with those who have not. Now, this certainly does not mean that people of different faiths should not interact. The people of Jesus are meant to love everyone, even their enemies. Christians should be coworkers, neighbors, and friends with all kinds of people. Paul's intention here is certainly not a call to isolationism. Rather, this is about the most intimate of relationships—binding your life together with another life. This should only be done with someone who is going the same direction you are headed!

If you are a believer, that means you live by faith. Faith in who? The Lord. So what does that mean? It means I believe what he says life is about and how to best live it. So I obey him, follow him, and embrace his perspective on all of reality and I engage everything in my life—from relationships with people to finances to my body to sexuality—in a way that pleases him. Now if you are not a believer, are you doing that? No. You may think Jesus was a good man, but you are not calling him the Lord of your life and striving to put all areas of your life under obedience to his Word. You may just be trying to be happy or to be a good person. Or you could be pursuing wealth or fame or power. Or maybe you are wandering aimlessly in life. I don't know. But whatever you are doing, I think we would both agree you are not striving to glorify the Lord Jesus Christ in all things. So, for goodness' sake, it makes no sense to bind yourself with someone who is. While the believer is trying to follow the Lord, the nonbeliever is pursuing his or her own interests, where one of two results will inevitably occur. First, one of you will give in and eventually follow the other. Often this means the believer abandons a pursuit of God and adopts a lifestyle that reflects no allegiance to God. Or second, you will both stubbornly pursue your agendas and neither of you will get where you want at the pace you want to and you will constantly frustrate each other. So one will eventually give in and die a little inside, or you will go spinning apart in divorce because your marriage bond can't handle the strain of your conflicting pursuits. Either way, you will both miss out on the joy of being linked together with someone who is running the same direction as you. This is the great joy in marriage: linking hands with someone and running after the same goal together. We'll talk more about that in the marriage section, but thinking about it needs to begin while you are dating.

My concern for some of you is that you are nervous about whether or not God will provide a man or woman who will love you. I fear that you will be tempted to drop your standards and be willing to date someone because they are hot and nice and because being connected to them makes you feel valuable. What concerns me is the inevitable result: you will be led into a way of living that does not please God and, therefore, will not ultimately bring joy to you. Too many times I have witnessed the sobs of those who married someone for looks and charisma and—after the flames of infatuation have died down—

> **Build other people up for the glory of God.**

find that they are bound to someone with whom they have very little in common. I want better for you. Please don't settle.

Some of you may respond, "Well, the person I'm interested in is not technically a Christian, but they believe in God. That's good, right?" Let me say this: some variety in marriage is great. You want some differences. She likes Pilates. You like racquetball. That's wonderful. But in the major course-determining factors in life you do not want to be asking the question, "What's the minimum we have to agree on?" When it comes to the most critical questions in life—Where did we come from? Why are we here? What is wrong with us? How is it dealt with? Where is all of history going? What happens after I die?—you want to agree on as much as possible. Don't settle for the fact that you both assent to the existence of a supreme being. Link up with someone with whom you share a deep commitment to God the Father, who sent God the Son to be the substitutionary atonement of our sins and to give us God the Holy Spirit as a deposit, working in us righteousness as we love one another and journey toward the day when faith will become sight and we will rejoice in perfect unity with the Trinity. You want that! Don't bind yourself together with someone who cannot converse with you about the deepest issues in life. The words of Tommy Nelson are true: "The loneliness of being single will not be assuaged by loneliness in a king-sized bed, laying next to someone who cannot communicate with you about the biggest issues in life."[5] Do not settle. In your heart set apart Christ as Lord and do not even consider linking your life up with someone unless he or she has an identical commitment. Paul told Timothy to "flee youthful passions and pursue righteousness, faith, love, and peace, along with those who call on the Lord from a pure heart" (2 Timothy 2:22). This is what you want: a pursuit of God alongside a person who is as passionate about him as you are.

Pursuing Allegiance, Not Preference

Let's take it a step farther. You not only want a believer in God, but a pursuer of God. Anybody can say they love Jesus; that's not hard. A friend of mine in college was sexually assaulted on a first date with a guy who had a Bible on his coffee table and a Christian bumper sticker on his car. Be careful. You do not want somebody who just slaps "Christianity" on his or her chest. When I was in college, I remember watching guys who were players incorporate more religious language when they were hitting on "good Christian girls." Beware. You do not want to date a guy or a girl who is just playing games with God. As a country friend of mine says, "You can put a bow tie on a turd, but it's still a turd." It does not matter to me one bit if someone regularly sits in church, posts on social media about being blessed, or gets a big tattoo of a Bible verse on their body. You need to watch their life over a period of time. You want to be able to see the *why* behind the decisions they make. The motivation you want to see is that they desire to please the Lord. You want to date someone who is submitted to the Lord's will. They are not perfect, but they are actively seeking him and trusting that he will make them more like him. You want someone with a low sin tolerance in their own lives. They want to grow more loving, more thoughtful, more truthful, and more courageous. That drive comes from within— the prompting of the Holy Spirit working in their life.

Why do you want a person like this? The reasons are multiple, but I will give you just two:

You want the benefit of their wisdom.

Marrying a wise person will allow you to navigate life well. The book of Proverbs states that fear of the Lord is the beginning of wisdom (9:10). Wisdom is an understanding of how the world works and an ability to work within it well.[6] Where does this wisdom come from? It begins with a fear of the Lord. When someone believes God made this place, they also believe that the way he tells us to work within the world will work best. That's why the fear of the Lord is the beginning of wisdom. No one understands a creation better than the one who created it. When I listen to God's Word on how to work within the world he made, I am set up to succeed.

Ladies, Psalm 1 declares that a man who delights in the law of the Lord will be "like a tree firmly planted by streams of water, which yields its fruit in its season and its leaf does not wither; and in whatever he does, he prospers" (v. 3 NASB). Wouldn't you like to be married to someone who prospers even when life is difficult? Get with a man who fears the Lord!

Men, listen to this description of a godly woman in Proverbs 31:

Strength and dignity are her clothing, and she smiles at the future. She opens her mouth in wisdom, and the teaching of kindness is on her tongue. She looks well to the ways of her household, and does not eat the bread of idleness. Her children rise up and bless her; her husband also, and he praises her, saying: "Many daughters have done nobly, but you excel them all." Charm is deceitful and beauty is vain, but a woman who fears the LORD, she shall be praised. (vv. 25–30 NASB)

Don't you want to be connected with a girl like that? Don't settle for, "Well . . . she works out a lot. She seems cool." You want a woman who fears the Lord! She will have an anchor of confidence in the Lord that will keep her from being unmoored by anxiety. She will give good advice when you need to process decisions, and she will speak to you with gentleness when she challenges you. She will have an industry about her labors in the home and outside of it that will serve to encourage your children, not discourage them. You will get up every day exclaiming, "Thank you, Lord, for this woman!" You want a girl like this? Then find one who fears the Lord.

These wonderful characteristics we long to find in a mate are sourced in God. So the smartest thing you can do is to link up with someone who is tethered to the Lord. Anybody can dig deep into their own soul and summon the willpower to tolerate a difficult person for a few hours. But you want to be married to someone who possesses a far deeper well of resources than their own heart can provide. You want to be married to someone who calls upon the inexhaustible riches of the love, joy, and peace of God (Galatians 5:19–23). You want someone with character—not perfect, but perfect*able*, because he or she is submitted to the Lord and longs to do his will.

You want the peace of their integrity.

You want the person you choose to marry to have an anchor point of *love* and *morality* outside of what you offer them, so that your marriage can stay strong even when you are at your weakest.

Men, you want a woman like Brenda Roever. Not long after she married her husband, Dave, he was sent to serve in the U.S. military in Vietnam. There, he suffered horrible burns to his body and face from a phosphorus grenade. As he lay in the ICU in Japan, he watched as a woman visited her husband—also a burn victim—in the neighboring bed. She laid her wedding ring on the bed and said, "I can't be seen with you. You are an embarrassment." And she left him to die in that hospital bed. Dave was terrified that his wife would react similarly when she saw his mangled face. However, when Brenda arrived she walked straight to her husband, at the lowest moment in his life, kissed his face, and said, "Welcome home." That is what you want. A woman whose faithfulness to you is not anchored in the shifting sands of circumstance.

Ladies, if you will forgive the crude example, I want to paint for you a plausible scenario. If and when you decide to have a baby, you will go through a period of several weeks or months after the birth when sex will not be an option for you. Husbands refer to this as "the long winter." You want a man who has control of his sexuality now, so that when sex is off the table for a few months you don't have to worry about whether or not he is taking his desires to the Internet, a coworker, or elsewhere. You want a man who is making war on his lusts now for no other reason than his allegiance to Christ. If you marry a guy like that, when he goes on a work trip you won't suffer through sleepless nights wondering what he's up to in his hotel room. You will be able to rest in the security that comes from having a man with integrity.

Now are you going to find all this out about a person on date one? No! And, honestly, a dinner date with just the two of you may not be the most effective method of evaluating whether or not your date has character. Anybody can bluff their way through a one-hour interview. You may need to watch for a while and see them around other people they are not trying to woo. How do they treat the young, the old, or the unpopular? A lot of people can be charming when making first impressions. You want to know what is happening behind the scenes.

In 1 Timothy 5, Paul advised Timothy in choosing leadership of the church. He warned him:

> Do not lay hands upon anyone too hastily and thereby share responsibility for the sins of others; keep yourself free from sin. . . . The sins of some men are quite evident, going before them to judgment; for others, their sins follow after. Likewise also, deeds that are good are quite evident, and those which are otherwise cannot be concealed. (vv. 22, 24–25)

Some people will obviously be trouble and you will know it in the first five minutes. Others, you need to observe for a while to see what kind of character rises to the surface. In due time, their deeds, whether good or bad, will come to light. What you want to see is someone who is striving to do beautiful things for beautiful reasons.

When I first met my wife, Donna, I was not impressed with the fact that she led worship at churches. It also meant little to me that she wrote worship songs. Why? Because those activities could easily be pursued for selfish purposes. Intrinsic in those activities were incentives that were sufficiently desirable to prompt one to continue that activity. Attention! Popularity! Power! I didn't know her motive. Anybody can write a song about anything. A man helped in writing "Single Ladies (Put a Ring on It)" for goodness' sake! I needed to keep watching.

As I observed her life I saw her consistently pursue holiness outside of any perceivable external motivator. Just because she loved God she mentored young women and trusted the Lord with her finances. I saw a girl who wanted to pursue the things of God without the promise of wealth, glory, or power. That attracted me. You want a person like that! When you link up with that kind of person, when they stand at the altar and promise to be faithful to you, "for better or for worse," you won't stare into their face hoping that they're being sincere. You will know it.

You may need to watch their life for a while to discern character. But we'll cover that more in the next chapter. The point now: you want someone who is actively pursuing the Lord.

An internal drive toward love and holiness. You want that in a mate. Why? Because that mate will continue to look more like Jesus and manifest his qualities throughout life—whether you deserve to be treated well or not, whether you provide incentive or not. Because there will be times when you are being a selfish jerk, or your anxiety or fear in life will manifest in a moment of panic or embarrassing selfishness. You want someone who will love you through the chaos because they love Jesus. If all they've got to anchor their commitment to you is their enjoyment of what you offer, what happens in those seasons when you don't have much to offer?

Keeping the Same Pace

I certainly do not want to suggest that there are different tiers within the family of God. We are all children of God by grace alone. And yet within the family of God there are people at different times who are pursuing him with different levels of intensity. It is important to keep this in mind when dating someone. It's similar to running a race. At a marathon there may be tens of thousands who are in the race. Thousands of them will cross the finish line that day. Yet there are some who will do it in three hours and others who will need about twenty-four. If you are a six-minute mile guy, you do not want to throttle back to jog along with the twelve-minute miler. If you are a light jogger, you certainly do not want to try to keep up with the front runners either. As you begin spending time with someone you are attracted to, you will need to evaluate this. If your highest ambition is to lay your life down as a martyr on the mission field and they just want to find a nice church to attend on Sundays, you may not want to try to run together for the next twenty to thirty years. Ladies, if you have to beg him to go to church now, imagine how exhausted you'll be when you have to do that week after week for the rest of your life. Men, if she sees your allegiance to the Lord as a cute hobby, then she will not enthusiastically join you in leading at church. Ultimately, you cannot lead her where she is unwilling to follow. So be careful. Do not close your eyes and hope it all works out. Be smart. You will be tied together with this person for life. Are they moving the direction you want to go? Are they running at a pace that will challenge you without discouraging and destroying you?

Let me clarify. I do not necessarily mean that you are identical in your expressions or pursuit of the Lord. When I met Donna, I knew more about the Bible than she did. I still do. I promise that is not an arrogant statement! I am passionate about reading. I spent several years and several thousand dollars to go to seminary and learn how to read the Bible in its original languages. She is not wired like that. She is more likely to write a poem than parse a verb. She writes a song much more readily than she reads a textbook. But she matches me stride for stride in a desire to know God. And when it comes to fearlessly loving people, speaking the truth in love, and selflessly offering hospitality, she far outpaces me. So the expression of our passions for the Lord look a little different, but the fire is burning at the same temperature. You want this.

Chemistry

While a potential spouse must have a character shaped by God, character alone is not enough. You want to live out your years with someone who is not only faithful to God but a good fit for you. You want godly character *and* good chemistry. We are transitioning here from the three critical factors of character to four factors of chemistry that have some bend in them. In what follows there will be a spectrum on which you can land.

Theologically Compatible

Theology is simply the study of God and one's understanding of him as revealed in the Bible. And your personal convictions and beliefs about God matter in your relationship. Is one of you Catholic and the other Protestant? One Calvinist and the other Arminian? Or, how about Baptist or Episcopalian? What are your strong theological convictions? This will raise some serious issues far beyond simply where the wedding ceremony will take place. You may discover that you have significantly different answers to questions about the nature of authority in the church, the role of sacraments, and how exactly the grace of God operates in a human life. Now, for some of you this might not seem that critical on the first few dates. It may not even come up in conversation. But I promise it will become an issue as you get farther down the road. As you begin to consider building a family together, these issues will heavily impact how you raise your kids. One or both of you will have to bend considerably if this is going to work. Proceed cautiously here.

Is one of you expressive in worship and the other more conservative? This may be an area where you find it relatively easy to compromise. Yet, for some of you, it may be an area of significant strain. How passionate are you about the presence or absence of electric guitars in a worship service? How committed are you to pipe organs or liturgy? At some point, this is going to come out. As you consider journeying in life together, these conversations will need to come up. And you will need to evaluate how willing you are to compromise.

There are critical theological issues concerning which you cannot bend: the existence of the triune God, the dignity and depravity of humanity, the substitutionary death of the historical God-man Jesus Christ, and salvation by grace through faith. Beyond these there are other critical issues you may be able to disagree on and work through together. Yet I would caution you here. While you do not need to be lockstep on every issue, you do want to make sure you are aligned on both the issues that are the most critical and the issues about which you feel the most passionate. So you may easily bend on the style of church service you attend, but be clearheaded about the other issues. You want to be able to agree upon, celebrate, and champion as many issues as possible as it relates to the way you as a family worship and pursue the work of the Lord.

Socially Compatible

One thing I want to say up front: socially compatible does not mean identical. Thank the Lord. Nobody wants to be married to themselves; at least you shouldn't! Donna is considerably more outgoing than I am. I like people, but I tend to be more introverted.

She loves yard work. I can't stand it. She loves mellow, singer-songwriter music. I prefer rap. So I am by no means suggesting here that you must be the same. In fact, there are great benefits to being different from each other as you relate to each other socially. It can often provide a necessary counterbalance. Donna benefits from my bookishness. I benefit from her artistic expressions. So by *compatibility*, I do not mean *uniformity*.

What I do mean, quite simply, is this:

Do you like hanging out with each other?

I am amazed how often I encounter couples that have not pondered this question. Maybe they dated for years and are just used to each other. Or they were fooling around quite a bit physically and didn't bother to really consider whether or not they found each other interesting when in nonsexual contexts.

Here's a reality you need to grab hold of:

When you are married, most of your time together will not be spent having sex!

So it is important to ask the question: Do I find this person interesting to talk to? Most of your married life will be spent hanging out together. Riding in the car. Eating meals. Sitting on the couch. If you find that you do not have much to talk about, that's a problem. If you find most of what that person says uninteresting, that is also a problem. Looks tend to fade quite a bit faster than personality. If you're only with a person because he or she is eye candy, that has diminishing value. Make sure it's someone whom you enjoy spending time with. That does not mean you have to enjoy all the same hobbies. It's okay if you love to work out and he really doesn't. But you do have to figure out how much you bend there. If you come alive by hiking in the woods, and she hates the outdoors, you'll need to consider that. When Donna and I met I enjoyed running. She did not. But that wasn't really a huge issue for me. I also love hiking. If she had hated the outdoors, that may have been a problem. Neither of us were big spenders on clothes. That helped. If we had vastly different shopping or extracurricular habits, that could potentially be a source of strain. You will have to bend a bit here. Not everything will be a perfect match, nor should it be. But you'll have to ask the question: If I love New York and he longs to live in Dime Box, Texas, do we have a future? How much are you willing to bend?

Vocationally Compatible

One wants to be an investment banker in Houston. The other wants to be a missionary to Calcutta. That may be a problem. One wants to be a pastor. The other can't see herself as a minister's wife. Might be a deal breaker. These kinds of things often come up naturally in conversation, but can be awkward to dig into. Does he support her career goals, or does he hope to have a wife who will stay home with the kids? Does she want to be a stay-at-home mom, but he really wants the extra income of marrying a lawyer? Again, not all of this will surface in the first conversation. But it will come up, and an important aspect of evaluation is to ask the questions: Where is this person's life going? Am I willing to go there? Are their goals compatible with mine? If not, how far are you willing to bend? Some compromise is essential. But too much and you may both end up really frustrated because you feel unable to fulfill your mission in life. It is much easier to contemplate these issues before the wedding! And much joy comes when you find someone with whom you share not only common beliefs, but a similar sense of mission in life.

In college my sister found a growing passion to be a part of relief work in Africa. She saw the value of a medical degree in that pursuit, but found in herself little passion to be a doctor. She used her time in college to hone her obvious skills in counseling, and while in graduate school she met a young man who shared a passion for relief work in Africa, and was a doctor. So they married and moved to Madagascar, where they could both use their gifts to meet the physical, emotional, and spiritual needs of the people. My brother had a desire to enter the military, and along the way he met a young woman from a family with deep military connections. She understood the challenges and deeply respected the sacrifice it would entail. They are a tremendous force for good in their military community. I knew I wanted to be a minister. I met Donna, who had similar passions, and we now minister together, albeit with very different ministry skill sets. Your pursuits may not be identical, but they do need to be compatible. This is an important factor in discerning whether or not God has ordained this relationship.

Physically Compatible

Some of you might be saying, "Finally! I was afraid you were not going to put this on the list!" Others of you might be saying, "Wait, should this be on the list? Isn't that too shallow a concern for the true believer?" Let me say that asking the question "Are you attracted to someone physically?" is not a bad question to ask. Often in biblical texts about married couples, it remarks on the beauty or handsomeness of the people. The Bible seems to see some value in this. It is okay to be attracted to someone. Yet you never see this as the primary criteria upon which a marriage relationship is built. It is an acceptable question to ask; it is just not a great question to ask first. What I mean is, this should be a factor but it should not be *the* factor in determining whether or not you want to be with someone. Why? For the simple, obvious, yet still, in the moment, often overlooked reality that beauty fades. It is foolish to base your entire reason for dating someone on looks, something that is destined to diminish with time. You would not want this! Because what happens if you get in a car wreck and get disfigured? Or if you contract a disease that causes your weight to spiral out of control? You want someone who loves you for more than your body as it appears when you meet. Also, if your analysis of human beings is simply superficial, you will miss out on some wonderful people. King Saul in the Old Testament was a handsome guy, but a horrible, insecure, irrational, and destructive leader. King David was handsome, but a bit shorter and less distinguished. Yet he had courage and compassion. He was a warrior, a poet, and a great leader. If you were just judging by looks, Saul would win, but in the end, your life would be ruined. I'm not saying to marry someone you find repulsive, but I am saying you'd do well to marry someone who scores a ten on character and an eight on looks, rather than a ten in looks and a zero in character. Be smart.

Before we move on to the subject of how to date, let me reiterate that the points above are not a treasure map to follow to find our true love. Instead, they are a lens through which to evaluate fellow travelers. In the end, the happiest people are not those who are actively seeking a mate, but those who are actively seeking their Maker. When we choose the latter course, we open ourselves up to the experience C. S. Lewis describes in *The Four Loves*: "When the two people who thus discover that they are on the same secret road are of different sexes, the friendship which arises between them will very easily pass—may pass in the first half-hour—into erotic love."[7] But how exactly do we pass from fellow traveler to lifelong travel companion? That is the subject of our next chapter.

5

how to date

Several years ago I hiked down into the Grand Canyon with a few good friends. We spent a day descending into the canyon below, camped for another full day at the bottom, then hiked back out on the third day. I awoke that second day with a passion to see a fifty-foot waterfall that I had read about. This would require a six-mile hike deeper into the canyon, then a six-mile trek back to camp before nightfall. My buddies did not love this idea. They wanted to relax in the river all day. I was not thrilled about the thought of walking to the falls by myself, but I decided to start walking toward the waterfall for a while and see what happens. As I strolled along I felt fantastic, so I decided to just keep going until I reached my destination.

But then, after what felt like a long time, I began to wonder, *Exactly how far along am I?* I realized I did not bring a watch or phone or anything to track my progress. So I began to get nervous. *What if I run out of water while I'm alone in the wild? What if this takes too long and I have to hike back in the dark? Should I turn back now? But I might already be close!* I decided the best thing to do was to speed up the process. I began to power walk.

Moments later, I caught up to a friendly young couple. It turns out they were headed to the same waterfall as part of their extended backpacking trip through the canyon. They invited me to join them, but I declined. I felt they would slow me down. So I sped ahead.

But as I raced on, a new fear surfaced: *What if I've already passed it? Surely I should have seen it by now. What if I'm just moving aimlessly into the wild, and the last anyone ever sees of me is the couple watching me speed-walk into oblivion?!* At this point panic set in. I freaked out. The thought shot into my mind, *I need to find my bearings. I must get to higher ground!* I began to scramble up the side of the cliff. In the midst of my ascent, I came charging around a bush and startled a deer. Maybe it's better said that we startled each other. He leapt back and I fell backward into a bush that drove a two-inch thorn deep into the palm of my hand. Tumbling back down the side of the canyon, I arrived back on the trail covered in dust and blood. At that moment, I suddenly heard the not-so-distant roar of descending water. Once I got to my feet again and began walking, I rounded a corner and looked up to see a gorgeous waterfall. Then I looked down and saw the sweet couple I had passed earlier, enjoying their lunch at the base of the waterfall. Unable to hide their surprise at my late, bloody, and dirty arrival, they asked, "What happened to you?" I realized there was no way to save face. I had to tell them that I had panicked and run around like a crazy person. The girl asked sweetly, "But didn't you see the huge sign that said 'waterfall'?" We all laughed about my misfortune, and then we passed the next hour eating the food they had brought while they bandaged me up.

Why tell you all of this? To illustrate a simple reality. The young couple and I got to the same destination, but I took a way less efficient and not-so-fun route to get there. This accurately illustrates modern dating.

People are finding love. It is happening every day. Yet it is undeniable that today the journey is taking considerably longer. In past generations the trails were more clear, the pathways better marked. Now we are all forging through the wilderness with no equipment, no guide, and only half a granola bar. We are making it, but we're getting pretty beat up along the way.

David Brooks, a columnist for the *New York Times*, wrote an article about the daunting social frontier facing the young, modern single. He explained,

> They hit puberty around 13 and many don't get married until they're past 30. That's two decades of coupling, uncoupling, hooking up, relationships, and shopping around. This period isn't a transition anymore. It's a sprawling life stage, and nobody knows the rules. Once young people came a-calling as part of courtship. Then they had dating and going steady. But the rules of courtship have dissolved. They've been replaced by ambiguity and uncertainty. Cellphones, Facebook and text messages give people access to hundreds of "friends." That only increases the fluidity, drama and anxiety.[1]

Watching this phenomenon from up close over the last decade has made me profoundly sad. Getting to know people, enjoying company over a good meal, falling in love: these experiences should be associated with words like *fun*, *exhilarating*, and *uplifting*. Yet far too often in my conversations with young people, the words associated with dating are *sad*, *exhausting*, and *stressful*. As someone who loves my young, single friends, I want a better journey for them.

And a better journey is possible! The path to love can be painful, but there is a way to navigate the process that can avoid a lot of needless pain. So if the last chapter was a description of the right kind of person to marry, in this chapter we'll walk through the most enjoyable and least painful *process* for how to find that person!

The Need for Process

The lack of any intentional dating process has created much of the distress in modern dating.

Girls lament, "He asked me to 'hang out.' Does that mean I'm going to be sitting around with him and his friends, or does that mean he is romantically interested in me?"

"Should I invest the emotional energy in evaluating this as a potential relationship?"

"What does *hang out* mean?!"

Yet at the same time, guys bemoan, "I don't know what I'm supposed to do."

"If I ask a girl out on a date it might sound too formal."

"If I really do just want to be nice and invite her to hang out with me and my friends, I don't know what connotations she puts with those words."

"It is just too much pressure."

"I'm out!"

And the spin cycle of chaos continues.

I remember visiting with one young woman who said in exhaustion, "I just wish everyone had a symbol on their forehead. All we would have to do is find the person with the matching symbol and then we'd know that is who we are supposed to marry." I will let you decide whether or not you think that would be a better system, but I sympathize with the frustration! What I can say definitively is that it does not work that way. The movement from singleness to marriage requires a journey through the process of evaluation.

In different cultures and at different times in history, that process of evaluation has been varied. The dominant form of evaluation in much of the world today is called *dating*. It is important to note that dating is a *process*. I keep coming around to that word because a process has movement to it. It's a series of actions unto a predetermined end. Dating is not a status that you sit in

> **Dating is more like crossing an ocean than it is like assembling a desk from IKEA.**

without any kind of momentum. You shouldn't say, "Well I guess we're dating," and just hang out there indefinitely. It's meant to have movement to an end—a destination called *marriage*.

The Bible does not talk about *dating* per se. As my friend Gregg Matte noted, there is no verse stating, "And Moses took Zipporah unto Chili's." However, the Scriptures do have much to say about how to evaluate relationships. So we can debate whether or not the modern system of dating is the best method for finding a mate. But I would rather focus on the principles laid out in Scripture concerning how to properly evaluate whether or not someone is a good fit. These principles are timeless. They apply across a broad range of cultures and scenarios. Specifically, I want to give you seven principles that can guide you through the process of dating.

The Ocean Versus IKEA

Before we begin it is important to note that what follows are principles, not steps. I have experienced that people tend to want steps more than they want principles. I can understand this. When I buy a desk at IKEA, I do not want them to hand me a book on general principles regarding the properties of wood and its relationship to metal implements. Rather, I want step-by-step instructions that tell me precisely how to assemble the desk. I don't want guidelines and theory; I want an exact pathway from desklessness to desk. But dating does not work this way. Human relationships are much too dynamic. Dating is more like sailing across the ocean than it is like assembling a desk from IKEA. Steps won't work when you are crossing the ocean on a boat. You cannot get turn-by-turn directions. The environment is too dynamic. Someone could give you a step-by-step book, but it would just be a history lesson of what worked that one time they crossed the ocean. Who knows what storms *you* will encounter along the way? Principles, however, may save your life. Knowledge of how to chart according to the stars. A compass to show you true north. A map. A sextant. The tools you need and the principles you must know to equip you to handle any challenge that comes up along the way. That information will get you from the shores of singleness to the port of marriage. The good news is that these guiding principles—if you apply them to your dynamic environment—will aid you in your journey. They can lead you safely through the tempestuous waters of dating.

Seven Principles for How to Date

1. Prayerfully

We must date prayerfully. Why begin here? Because with prayer we invite the God of the universe into the process with us. And resting in the sovereign love of God takes the desperation out of dating.

I have found that many of the actions (or lack thereof) in

dating are driven by fear. The fear of being rejected. The fear of being alone. This fear can drive us to date someone we know we shouldn't date. Or to act in unnatural ways or say awkward things because we are painfully self-conscious or trying hard to win someone over. The process of evaluation gets scrambled because no one is relaxed enough to be themselves! Anxiety motivates action, but like my trek in the Grand Canyon, not often the best action.

This is what makes prayer at the outset so critical. When we pause to acknowledge God in the process, we allow the truth about who he is to influence our thoughts and actions. If we are in the clutches of fear, we are more prone to try to manipulate situations to make ourselves look better. But when we remember that Romans 8:28 declares, "We know that God causes all things to work together for good to those who love God, to those who are called according to His purpose" (NASB), it frees us from the terror of being alone—which, alone, has the ability to drive us to compromise our standards. It liberates us from constantly trying to dress or act in a way that wins someone's attention. If I am resting in God's guidance of my future, I am free to be a servant and a friend to the people around me. I can relax and enjoy every moment of my life because I rest in the knowledge that my strong and loving God is leading me in a good way. We don't get to know everything in this life, but we do get to know the One who knows everything, and that is an encouraging thought.

Do you trust God with your dating life? He is not only strong enough to guide your story, he is compassionate enough to want to take your fears from you. First Peter 5:7 invites you to, "Cast all your anxiety on him because he cares for you" (NIV). You can trust him with your anxieties and your dating future. He is strong enough to carry you and loving enough to want to. When we realize the sovereign Lord of the universe cares for us like this, we will be able to relax and function without fear. We are free to make good decisions and to take action in a way that blesses others. This is an invaluable asset in dating.

When I get that vertical connection clear—a connection with the strong God who is loving—then I can see people as precious creations in his image, not to use but to honor. Then, as a part of honoring people, provide clarity.

2. Clarity

So let's say you are running along, pursuing the things of God, and you see someone who seems cute and fun running along at the same pace. Or, to step out of the running metaphor, let's say you are involved in a community of believers in Jesus. You are involved with a church and with ministries that serve the needs of your town or city. You are going to brunch with your group of friends, and somewhere in that mix you meet someone you think you want to get to know a little better. What should you do?

Answer: initiate with clarity.

Ephesians 4 says that a hallmark of the people of Jesus is that we "[speak] the truth in love" (v. 15). Proverbs 24:26 declares that an honest answer is a kiss on the lips. It is a sign of respect and love to tell someone the truth. Now, honesty does not mean a full disclosure of every thought in your head. Proverbs celebrates prudence, the careful discerning of our words. Sometimes the first thought that pops into your head is not really what you believe or think, and definitely not what you should say. Yet, in the world of dating and relationships, ambiguity is the seedbed of anxiety. And what the world needs now is some clarity.

Proverbs 29:18 declares, "Where there is no vision, the people perish" (MEV). The word *perish* there can also be translated "unrestrained" or "disturbed" or "out of control." This is modern dating. When there is no leader giving clear direction—expressing, "We are going this way"—people feel out of control, disturbed, and anxious. Think about the last time you were riding in a car and someone asked, "Where are we?" That statement is not normally accompanied with happy feelings. It is not fun being lost. It is not life-giving. This is true in dating as well. In fact, much of the anguish in modern dating could be alleviated if we mustered the courage to graciously tell each other what we think, how we feel, and what we would like to do. It is a lack of leadership that is killing the joy in dating. We need clarity. And we need clarity in three important ways.

- You need clarity in initiation.

This continues to be a challenge for and responsibility borne in large part by men. In 2012, a national survey indicated that only 12 percent of American women asked anyone out the previous year.[2] So whatever you believe about male-female roles in relationships, the data continues to suggest that women want men to initiate. Research also suggests that women prefer men ask them out in person. The preference of being asked by text comes in second, though some do not like it. Calling on the phone comes in third, with some not preferring that either. So good luck if you want to initiate by text or call, boys. No telling if that will be a hit or a miss.

I read these polls and wondered myself if they were really true. So I put together a few focus groups and was amazed to hear the data consistently come in the same. Men, the verdict is in: women want you to ask them out, and they would prefer you do it face-to-face.

I also discovered that women almost universally hate being invited to "hang out." I was personally surprised by the looks of revulsion that language received. Why the strong reaction? Girls did not like the lack of clarity associated with being asked to "hang out." So I asked the question, "What would you prefer a man say? Would you like him to use the word *date*?" Honestly, I thought they would shy away from that word. I assumed, as have many men I have visited with, that the language "Would you like to go on a date with me?" sounded too formal or would seem too intense for a generation that exudes reticence to settle down. To my surprise, the women I met with unanimously said "Yes!" One responded, "Use the word *date*, so then at least I know what I'm getting into." Another added, "If using the words 'I would like to ask you on a date' feels too weird, then plan something and then invite me to that thing." Over and over again I heard the same thing from women. They want men who are interested in them enough to initiate something more formal than just "hanging out."

- Women and men alike want clarity in the process.

I have certainly seen this desire for clarity play out in my own dating experience. When I dated girls in college, I confused every one of them. I was not sure how to express my feelings. Heck, I was not even sure what my feelings were! I finally had to take a break from romantic relationships altogether. I had to get "me" sorted out a bit more before I could try to get a "we" off the ground. But by the time I met my wife-to-be, Donna, things had changed. I felt more confident in the Lord's leadership of my life and more comfortable with myself. I met her at a ministry function where we were both serving, and I ran into her a few times later in larger group settings. I watched the way she treated people. She was gracious. She was kind. She was fun. I thought to myself, *I think I am attracted to this girl.* A large group of our mutual friends were going out to a movie, so I approached her and asked if she would like to join us. She agreed. So we went and I made sure I sat by her. It was not a date, but it provided a great opportunity for us to spend a little more time together.

After that I called her and said, "Hey, my brother is in town. He's got this New Year's Eve thing he's going to. He invited me to join him and I need a date. Would you like to come with me?" I felt that this was a way to get some more time with just her, away from our social spheres, but that would also provide her the comfort of knowing there would be other people there. She said yes. We had a great time. At the end of the night, before she got out of the car, I told her, "Tonight was fun. Can I call you again?" I said this to her because I did not want her to get out of the car and then have a few days of wondering whether or not I had a good time, whether or not I would ever talk to her again, should she reach out, or should she wait to hear from me. I had been around enough women by this point in my life to know that the time of ambiguity is uncomfortable. I wanted to leave her with some clarity so that she could walk away from the date thinking, *He had fun. He will call. There is less to analyze and nothing to plan. He has given me an idea of what comes next.*

As our dating life continued, I tried to always end every evening with something along the lines of these two sentences: "This was fun. I will call you." That way she was never left guessing on what would happen next. Then, every few weeks, before she got out of the car after an evening together, I would initiate a longer conversation. It usually consisted of me saying something like, "I just want you to know, I am really enjoying getting to know you and would like to continue spending time with you. I am not in a place where I am trying to get married in the next six months, but I am also not simply wasting your time either. I could see this relationship going further. So I would like to keep calling you if you are interested." She told me later how much she appreciated this. "I always knew where I stood," Donna would tell me. We can give each other the gift of freedom from anxiety through the simple act of providing clarity.

- You need to offer clarity about how to exit.

We also must be clear with each other about how this process of dating might end. I would suggest that, within the conversation about how you would like to continue seeing him or her, say something like, "I want you to know that if at any point you don't feel comfortable with this, please let me know. You have every right to say that to me and we can be done. I trust the Lord with my life. I trust the Lord with your life. So if in any way this feels off or uncomfortable to you, then we will just stop. No pressure." We need to provide each other with a clear door out. In 1 Corinthians 14 Paul declared, "God is not a God of confusion but of peace" (v. 33). We are meant to be like this as well. When we give people clarity, we give them peace. How do we give them clarity? When John tried to succinctly describe Jesus, he kept coming back to the refrain that he was "full of grace and truth." We should all strive for this: graciously speaking the truth to one another.

Ladies, this applies to you as well. As often as I talk with young women who are confused about the lack of clarity in the process of courtship, I speak to just as many men who describe the anxiety of not knowing if a girl likes them or not. Don't just freeze a guy out and never respond to his text. Ghosting is neither godly nor gracious! Give him the courtesy of a response, even if it feels potentially awkward. If you aren't interested, say something like, "You know, you seem like a great guy, but I just can't see this going anywhere. But thank you for the invitation."

I talked with a young man who told me that a girl he had asked out said those exact words to him. As he told the story to a group of men and women, we were all dying to know how that kind of honesty felt. He said, "It was such a relief. Sure I was disappointed, but I did not have to waste time guessing what she thought." She honored him by providing a gracious, honest explanation. Gentlemen, women say the same. I remember visiting with a young woman in the months prior to her wedding. I will never forget what she said to me about her dating experience. She confided, "I loved the clarity he gave me. Every couple of dates he would talk a bit about where we were." She added, "I always knew where I stood. I did not have to guess what he thought."

Believers in Jesus do not need to play games. *I'll flirt a little tonight, but then I'll wait to text until two weeks later.* That kind of thinking is for people with nothing better to do. If you are a Christian, then you believe this world is going to hell, but in the midst of the tragedy we have the remedy. We know the Hero of the story and we've been given a few short years to leverage every bit of influence we have to spread the message that life is available in him. We don't have time to mess around with people's emotions. Say what you mean. Mean what you say. Be clear about the process.

So we're prayerful with clarity, but always with a sense of autonomy.

3. Autonomy

Much of the angst in dating stems from viewing dating as a status rather than a process.

The Bible acknowledges a few relational categories. The first distinction lies between those who trust in Jesus Christ and those who do not. The Bible is very clear here: you do not date across these lines because you have different allegiances and different directions. Now, there are many verses in the Bible concerning how the people of Jesus are meant to reach out relationally across that boundary. We love those who do not believe. We extend kindness and generosity across that boundary. Our primary goal in those exchanges is to do all we can to help them see, understand, desire, and embrace an eternal relationship with God, not a romantic relationship with us.

There is also a significant divide within the community of Jesus. When you come to faith in Jesus, you not only begin a new relationship with God as a father but also gain all other believers as brothers and sisters. We are part of a family. There are a host of Bible verses concerning how we are to treat members of this community. When you cross the line of entering a covenant of marriage with one person until death do you part, you enter into a narrower circle with just the two of you. Now there are another set of Bible verses concerning how you are to treat that one person. When you step into a covenant together, a whole world of privileges and responsibilities open up to you that should not be a part of your relationship with a brother or sister in Christ.

But here is where the problem lies: in our culture today, we want to create a separate, interim category called "we're dating." We want to enter a sphere entitled "boyfriend and girlfriend." What we try to communicate when we announce those labels is, "We are not just brother and sister; we want to be more than that. But we are not married. We do not want to take on all of that weight. We are something else—a hybrid—that gives us certain responsibilities and affords us certain privileges." In essence, we attempt to make "dating" a status we rest in rather than a process we move through.

When you create this separate category, the question immediately rises, "What are the rules?" As we try to enter the sphere of dating someone, we tend to bump into the "rules" as the other person understands them. You can usually spot them in statements that include the phrase "supposed to." Example:

"Hey, why didn't you text me today?"

"What? Uh, I don't know."

"You're supposed to text me."

"I'm supposed to? I didn't know that."

"Yeah, you're my boyfriend. You are supposed to text me every day."

Or, "Hey, are we going out tonight?"

"Well, no. I'm going out with my girlfriends."

"What? Why didn't you make plans with me? I thought we were supposed to hang out on weekends."

"So, I am supposed to check with you first?"

"Well, yeah. I'm your boyfriend."

"I'm sorry. I didn't know that 'rule.'"

Then one person gets defensive and hurt. The other feels the need to apologize, but isn't entirely sure what line they crossed. What is going on here? We are bumping into a new set of responsibilities because of moving into the culturally created sphere of boyfriend and girlfriend. Each person is establishing a law—an official code of conduct for the boyfriend-girlfriend relationship.

The same thing happens with privileges. A Christian man will understand that when a girl is simply his Christian sister, he is not allowed to touch her in certain ways. But once she enters the sphere of girlfriend, a new world of access to her body opens up. He might think, *I can touch her rear. Maybe not grip it while we walk through the mall together. That's weird. Just at her apartment or something. Maybe while we're watching a movie and my arm is around her waist and it suddenly gets sooo tired that it has to fall into cheek range. I can do that now because she's my girlfriend.* Or maybe, *My tongue gets to go in her mouth now because she is my girlfriend.* You get the idea. We create this new sphere and we put into it certain responsibilities and privileges.

There's only one problem: God does not recognize this status.

You are either brother and sister or you are husband and wife. There is no intermediate sphere.

This is where so many young people get confused. We make dating a status rather than a process. *If I can just enter this status, I get certain responsibilities and certain privileges. I can hang in this zone for a while, enjoying as many of the perks as I can while staving off the harsher responsibilities of marriage.* It sounds like a sweet deal, yet this is where so many get hurt. This is where so many questions arise. We are trying to create a way of relating outside of God's economy, and we are finding that it does not work very well.

So many of the questions I receive about dating fail to make any sense if you come to understand dating as a process of evaluation. I had someone ask me, "My boyfriend and I have been dating for years. How do we keep the love alive?" I had no idea how to answer that. If by dating him you are evaluating whether or not you want to marry him, and if you find him boring, then that's your answer. So don't marry him! The goal of dating is not to make someone conform to a standard you have imposed. It is to assess what kind of person he or she is and discern whether or not the two of you are a fit.

Someone else will ask me, "I've been dating this girl for a while and I think she should start going to church with me now. How do I tell her that she's supposed to do that?" Supposed to? I have no idea where it is written that she has to go to church with you. If she has no interest in getting involved at church, then that is a helpful piece of information in your evaluation. That won't suddenly change if you get married. But if you are not her husband, she has no obligation at all to follow you anywhere. Her life is her own. She can go to whatever church she wants. Now, if you get married, you two will need to work that out together. But there are no biblical obligations for a status called *dating*.

The most common questions revolve around what is permissible physically. How far is too far? The married man has clear biblical texts concerning physicality: "May you enjoy her breasts forever" (Proverbs 5:19, author paraphrase). That's a command! The brother and sister in Christ have clear commands as well. In 1 Timothy 5 Paul commanded young Timothy, "Treat older women as mothers, younger women as sisters with absolute purity" (v. 2, author paraphrase). What about the boyfriend and girlfriend? There are no verses for that category because God does not acknowledge that as a category. So if you are dating, your operative verses are 1 Timothy 5. Then the question becomes, "How far is too far with your mom? Where is the line with your sister?" I would submit you do not fool around with your sister, because that is nasty. In the same way, the Bible draws a hard boundary between what is permissible sexually. In marriage: much. In singleness: none. In dating: still none!

I have had some say, "Well, Ben, we've been dating a long time. It is like we are married." No. It's not. When you consider the gravity of the covenant of marriage—the fact that you are committing to someone to unite your finances, family, and future forever—you realize that is a very different level of weight. A dating relationship, no matter how long it may have gone on, can be dissolved in an hour. Marriage opens up a whole new world of privileges because it also requires shouldering a whole new world of responsibilities. So if someone is saying to you, "I want the privilege of access to your body, but I don't want the responsibility of loving and caring for you forever," that is not a covenantal love. True love does not request access to your body while simultaneously avoiding any responsibility to care for you emotionally and financially. Try to make it sound as romantic as you want, but it is a selfish endeavor and God does not acknowledge it as honorable.

In marriage the two become one. A dramatic reorienting takes place. But until that covenant happens, you are still two. You are separate. That means there is a measure of separation in your decisions. You are accountable before God for your own life.

When someone says to me, "I have been talking with this girl for a while. We're trying to figure out when to make it official, like, Facebook official. What's your advice?" I always ask in response, "Are you, as an individual, in an emotional, spiritual, and financial situation where you feel you could reasonably get married in the next six months?" Normally the guy answers, "No." I respond, "Then you do not need to be in a rush to try to lay some claim on this girl. You do not need to expedite attempting to name your relationship. Because what you are trying to do is get the security and comfort of locking her down, saying to the world, 'She is MY girlfriend.' But what does that mean? It means other guys can't have her. It means you have laid a certain claim on her. But under God, you have no rights over her! She can do whatever she wants!"

When I was dating Donna, I told her all along, "You have to make your own decisions under God, of where you are going to go, how you are going to serve, and what you will do. I am really enjoying getting to know you, and I could see us moving into marriage, but until that day we must each make our own decisions." The tension of knowing she had complete freedom to leave at any time forced me to prioritize the process of really evaluating whether or not we were a fit. Knowing that there is a barrier of separation between us made me think seriously about my willingness to cross the line from brother/sister in Christ to husband/wife until death do us part. For me, a bit of a slow processor, this evaluating took about a year. After that, when I was convinced that life with her would be better than life without her, I did not delay getting a ring. That's what you want—a season of real evaluation that leads to a solid conclusion: either we are a good partnership or we are not.

Dating is not a way of maximizing benefits and minimizing obligations. It is not romantic to waste each other's time. Date to evaluate, and evaluate as quickly as you can but as long as it takes.

Now, for those of you thinking, *Oh no, I already have a boyfriend. Or, I have a girlfriend. We are going to have to break up now.* Let me say that I honestly do not care if you use the word *boyfriend* or *girlfriend*. What I do care deeply about is what you *mean* when you say those words. Be honest with yourself and with each other. If by *boyfriend* or *girlfriend* you mean, "This buys me certain privileges and access to this person," then I am telling you, it does not. Not under God. So you can use the terms *boyfriend* and *girlfriend*. But make sure as you do, you keep in mind, and remind each other, "I have no right to this person's body. I have no claim on this person's life. This person is not mine. She is a daughter of God and my sister in Jesus and I will treat her as such. He is a son of God and my brother in Jesus and I will treat him as such."

You may be asking, "But what exactly does that look like?" I believe the following principles for dating will help to clarify that.

4. Purity

Some of you may be asking, "In today's modern age why should we remain sexually pure while dating?" I have heard this question sincerely presented by a number of young people. Is sexual purity realistic in this day and age? Is it even healthy?

There is much we need to say about sexuality. So much in fact that we have dedicated an entire chapter to this issue. But for our purposes here, it is important to note that the introduction of sex into a dating context sabotages the evaluation process.

In 1 Corinthians 6, Paul spoke about this, saying, "Do you not know that he who is joined to a prostitute becomes one body with her?" (v. 16). This sounds like an obvious statement. If someone "joins" with a prostitute, of course they unite bodies. So what's the point, Paul? The point is that Paul meant much more by "one body" than we may understand. Paul followed this assertion by quoting the Old Testament, "the two will become one flesh" (v. 16). What he was saying is that sex is far more than just physical contact. A much deeper, emotional bonding takes place.

Anthropologist Helen Fisher explains, "Casual sex isn't so casual. With orgasm you get a spike of dopamine. Dopamine's associated with romantic love, and you can just fall in love with somebody who you're just having casual sex with. With orgasm, then you get a real rush of oxytocin and vasopressin—those are associated with attachment. This is why you can feel such a sense of cosmic union with somebody after you've made love to them."[3]

You can imagine how this can completely distort the process of evaluating whether or not someone is a good companion for life. In the Old Testament, the word *hallup* is often used to describe a husband and wife. A great translation of that word is "best friend." Your spouse is meant to be your best friend. The process of dating, done correctly, helps us evaluate whether or not you have that kind of connection with someone. But if you introduce sex into the relationship early, your mind gets shot with happy chemicals that makes you addicted to their body. You get hooked on the sexual experience with that person, and begin to lose the ability to properly evaluate whether this person is someone you like hanging out with.

Many of you have seen this happen with friends. You see a couple together and think, *Why are they together? They have so little in common. They don't seem to enjoy each other's company. They enjoy so few similar interests.* Often, all they have keeping them in the relationship is the physical aspect. And it is a strong incentive. Why? Because sex is built to be a bonding experience. It is designed by God to bond you to someone. But if you introduce it too early before you've evaluated whether or not you enjoy spending time with this person, you have set yourself up for serious disappointment. As time goes by and the sex becomes normalized, the buzz wears off. Then what do you have left? For many people, they find themselves bonded to someone they do not like very much or who they would not want their children to be like. I don't want this for you.

When you throw sexuality into a relationship too quickly, it distorts your ability to evaluate whether or not this person is a good friend. It makes you stay longer in relationships you shouldn't be in, and it makes the breakups so painful. I have counseled scores of young people who have admitted to me through tears that their deepest pain comes from the fact that they gave so much of themselves to somebody, and it wasn't the right somebody. So be careful. Wait. Don't arouse and awaken love until it pleases.[4]

You may question, "Ben, won't this lack of sexual fulfillment in a dating relationship create tension?" My answer: YES! Yet that tension is meant to propel you through the process of evaluation. "Will restraint be difficult?" Yes! But it is far better than the pain of the alternative. Science and the Bible agree: all the physical coupling and decoupling we do is infinitely harder on us than the discipline of learning restraint.

You may also be wondering, *Okay, so if we are not fooling around, then what exactly are we doing if we are on a date?* That takes us to our next point.

5. Graciously

Let's say you are attracted to someone and you discover that they are interested. Now what? Do you suddenly become a salesman entering an extended marketing campaign to convince someone to love you? Or must you transform into an endlessly creative romantic, constantly stoking the flames of passion? Or, on the other end of the spectrum, do you commit to changing nothing about your behavior, in an attempt to preserve the "real you"? In the name of authenticity you declare that, "I am not going to dress up, make plans, or put forth any effort whatsoever. I am just going to sit on the couch and watch TV, and if she doesn't like it, I'll say, 'Too bad. This is me being real. Get used to it.'" Is that what we are meant to do?

Let me answer that with a resounding "no." You should put some effort in. Yet you should not suddenly take on a whole new role and set of responsibilities. But I would affirm that our identity determines our activity. Who we are informs what we do. So who are you when you are on a date? If you are a believer in Jesus, then you are a reconciled, adopted child of God. You are a son or daughter of the King of heaven. And while you are on a date, so is the person sitting across from you.

So how do you deal with a child of royalty? That's simple: with courtesy. The word *courtesy* means to behave with manners that fit a royal court. In time it came to mean politeness, respect, and kindness. This is a great perspective. If I am asking someone who has trusted in Jesus out on a date, I am dealing with the child of the King and should do all I can to treat this person in a courteous manner.

Incidentally, this is true whether the person identifies as a child of God or not. All human beings are created in God's image and worthy of honor. In high school I was propositioned sexually by a younger girl. I declined her advances. But it was not because she was not attractive. She was. And I didn't say no out of fear of her father, though he owned many guns. And I didn't do it out of fear of her brother, though he was a massive mountain of a human being. I said no out of reverence for God. If someone mistreats my daughter, they have a problem with me. If I mistreat a daughter of God, then God will have a problem with me. I did not want to dishonor him by using her, even if she was open to being used.

But what exactly does it look like to treat someone with courtesy? In his letter to the Ephesians Paul spent three chapters telling us about all that God had done to rescue, forgive, and adopt people into his family by the grace of Jesus. He then turned a corner in the last three chapters and gave more than forty commands on how the children of God, in light of his grace, are meant to treat one another. He declared that God has equipped us "for building up the body of Christ, until we all attain . . . to the measure of the stature of the fullness of Christ" (Ephesians 4:12–13). He explained that, "speaking the truth in love, we are to grow up in every way into him who is the head, into Christ" (v. 15). Paul stated here that as we intersect with one another, our words and actions should build up others so that they might be more like Jesus. This includes while we are on dates with another.

For my senior year of college, my sister began her freshman year at the same school. I remember sitting in the lunchroom one afternoon and some guys began to joke about how they were going to try to date my sister. I did not see it as funny at all, because I knew these guys and I knew they did not treat women very well. Sure they were smooth and charming, but at the end of the day the whole affair of wooing a girl was more about what they could get from her than what they could give. I told them there was absolutely no way they would ever get anywhere near dating my little sister. One of them laughed, "Ben, is anyone going to be good enough?" I said, "Of course. I'm not one of those guys who is going to hate every person who likes my sister. Someone will be worthy." But as I left the lunchroom, I pondered that question: *What would I want a guy to do if he had a chance to date my sister?* The answer sprang to mind immediately: I would want him to treat her in a way that, regardless of whether or not their dating ended in marriage, she would be a better person and more like Christ as a result of his influence. I would want him to do or not do whatever he had to in order to play a role in helping her be all she is meant to be under God. Then the thought entered my mind, *Ben, do you treat girls this way?* And I began to cry. I realized I didn't. I was not always encouraging. I was not always clear. And I did not always have the best intentions. From that day forward I made a vow to myself: *If I ever date a girl, regardless of whether or not we marry, I want her to be able to say, "I am a better person for having spent time in proximity to that man."* I believe that is a great aim in dating.

You want the net effect of your presence in any relationship to be that the other person is better—trusts and loves God more as a result of your presence in his or her life. If you leave a trail of broken hearts and confused people, then you need to evaluate what you're doing. Your aim should be to bless, not simply to impress. Your actions are more about blessing the other person than impressing him or her.

So go to dinner, but don't obsess about trying to get the other person to like you. Rather, get to know him or her. Do things you like doing: go rappelling, go for a run, or do a ministry event together. While you are doing it share what you are learning. You are not trying to win him or her over to like you; you are trying to evaluate if the two of you are a fit. But while you are doing that, listen intently, ask good questions, and share your thoughts honestly. Compliment. Encourage. And speak your mind with sincerity and kindness. Don't stress too much about trying to impress. Dating is for evaluating and blessing. That's it.

6. Community

If dating is a means of evaluation, it is wise to allow other people you trust in the conversation who can provide wisdom throughout the process.

Proverbs 11:14 states, "Where there is no guidance, a people falls, but in an abundance of counselors there is safety." Romantic feelings are intoxicating and at times distorting. In the throes of infatuation we can lose objectivity. Getting the right voices speaking into the process can keep you safe from spending too much time with the wrong person. Not only can they keep you from dating the wrong person, they can help you identify the right one. Proverbs 24:6 declares, "in abundance of counselors there is victory." Pairing off alone is good, but if you pair off alone too often, you may lose touch with a resource that can help you discern whether or not this is a good fit.

This is one of my greatest concerns about online dating. It eliminates this important contribution of the community. Between 2005 and 2012 more than one-third of couples who got married in the United States met through online dating. Online dating was the single biggest way people met their spouses. Bigger than work, friends, and school combined! Meeting in a "place of worship" was only 2.66 percent. Records have been kept since the 1940s, and the categories of "met through friends," "family," and "at church" have all declined significantly. (Church is almost nonexistent now; from 13 percent in the 1940s to 2 percent today.) Only two categories increased in percentage: bars and online.[5] My problem with this trend is that both of those places tend to eliminate the constructive voices of community. In online dating the selection process happens with just you and your screen. And in a bar often the conversation is so loud no one can really hear what you are saying to each other. In a bygone era, men used to have to come to a girl's house to court her. This was to keep the girl safe, in the event that the guy was a creep. But it was also to allow the girl's family and friends to evaluate the young man. Remove those voices, and the only person you have to give you information on the person is *the person* and that is a very biased source. Now, let me say here that I do not think it is wrong to meet someone online. However,

I would encourage you to get some people you know and trust to offer you wisdom and to speak into the process early and often. It could save you a lot of heartache.

> # God is strong enough to carry you and loving enough to want to.

It can also keep you safe. When Donna and I were dating, we did not want a lot of people to know initially. We both had relatively high-profile jobs, and we did not want a lot of people trying to influence our newly formed relationship. I did want some key voices providing feedback, however. I asked a few married friends to spend time with us. I selected friends that I knew loved God, loved me, and were not afraid to tell me exactly what they thought. Early on, some of them voiced some concerns. Later, as our relationship matured, it gave me increased confidence when those friends who were initially skeptical grew to be more enthusiastic about our relationship.

In time, as our relationship became more serious and marriage became a distinct possibility, our key friends moved even closer, to give us counsel, encouragement, and some accountability. Donna had a family friend who was a former Navy SEAL. He would frequently pull me aside and ask me how I was doing. He never accepted "fine" as an answer. He explained that he knew sexual purity was a temptation the closer a couple moved toward marriage, and he wanted to make sure I had proper safeguards with Donna. He would often corner me against a wall to persistently ask me how we were doing in this regard. He would then always give me a big hug and pray for me, often with tears in his eyes. His genuine concern for Donna always moved me, and I was so grateful for the accountability I had with him.

Several years ago I spoke to a gathering of young professionals from India. Though most of them did not have arranged marriages, they fully intended to have their parents deeply involved in the process. I remember listening with fascination as they marveled about the American way of dating. "Why would you not want your parents' voice in the process?" they would ask. Parents usually know their child well, have their best interest in mind, and can be the wisest people they know. Why would you eliminate their voice from the process? It's a great question. You may not have biological parents who can serve that role for you, but the community of Jesus can. Surround yourselves with godly counsel, and your chances of victory rise exponentially.

7. Patiently

There should be no rush into "until death do us part." Take the time to let the relationship grow at its own pace. In 1 Timothy 5:22, Paul warned Timothy, "Do not be hasty in the laying on of hands." Though this is a passage about leadership in the church, the principle can easily apply to dating. "Laying on of hands" here refers to conferring authority on someone. Paul warned Timothy not to be in a rush to do this. He explained that "the sins of some people are conspicuous, going before them to judgment" (v. 24). There will be some people who, within five minutes of meeting them, it is obvious that they should not be entrusted with a leadership role. They're loud, brash, cruel, or arrogant. Their reputation for damaging relationships precedes them. It is easy to see you should not put them in a position of authority.

For others, however, Paul noted that "their sins follow after" (v. 24 NASB). That means that for a few months they are going to look pretty good. They appear charming, polite, gifted, and gracious. It may seem like an easy call to put them in leadership. But over time some cracks begin to show in the veneer. Maybe they are kind as long as things are going their way, but a little bit of stress and they lash out. Or maybe they are working overtime to hide some addictive behavior. There are issues in their life that don't surface right away, but given time, they become visible. You want to make sure you have waited long enough to see how their character handles different challenges and seasons before you grant them the authority of leadership.

The same holds true in dating. Do not rush to put on a ring. Wait and watch someone's character. Some people will be obviously unsuitable for dating within the first five minutes of a conversation. They are insensitive, short-tempered, or perverted. Others will seem nice at first, but you need to give it time. Consider the movie *Frozen*. Prince Hans looked like a dream come true the first night Anna met him. A few hours of charming banter convinced the young princess that they were "meant to be." Love had opened the door! Yet a few acts later in the movie, he betrays her and leaves her to die. Be careful, ladies! Don't rush to marry a Prince Hans when a Kristoff might be just around the corner. Wait long enough to see character. Watch long enough to see how they react when things do not go their way. See how they treat people who they aren't trying to date. Give yourself the space to see them in every season. In the same way character flaws will show over time, Paul noted, "So also good works are conspicuous, and even those that are not cannot remain hidden" (v. 25). Just like defective character, quality character will not stay hidden.

The more I watched Donna, the more beautiful and noble I perceived her to be. Dating for more than a year allowed me to see her in a host of different scenarios, and even when she may not have initially reacted in the most positive way to stresses and strains, she always rose up and tried to do the very best thing to honor God and others. The longer I watched her manifest character, the more my confidence grew that my affections were aptly placed. In the first few months I realized that my attraction to her physically was coupled with a chemistry with her relationally. She could make me laugh. But over the next several months I saw that she had depth of character as well. As we spent time with our good friends, they saw it too. We were a great fit. And when the time was right, we walked down the aisle together.

Will this happen for you? I don't know. But I do know that God is a good Shepherd, and he will take care of us. He has given us wisdom in how to evaluate a potential mate, and he has given us himself to lean on as we journey through the life he has given us.

> It is better to take refuge in the LORD than to trust in man. It is better to take refuge in the LORD than to trust in princes. (Psalm 118:8–9)

I pray that God in his due time would bring you the right prince or princess to love you all your days. But I pray that your hopes in your season of singleness would not be fixed on a prince or a princess, but on the King. Walk with him, believing that he will care for your needs and, if it be his will, lead you to the right person in his good time.

6

sex

One summer I worked for my dad out in Beeville, Texas. The work consisted of a variety of seriously country tasks. Build a fence. Mow seven acres of grass. Herd the cattle I may have accidentally let out of the pen. For the uninitiated, South Texas easily reaches 100-degree temperatures during the summer. So this was serious, character-building kind of stuff. The sort of work that makes you never want to have to do work like this again. So I will never forget the day my dad came out and gave me a new assignment.

"Son, do you see that massive pile of brush out back?"

"Yes, sir. It is higher than the house."

"I want you to light it on fire."

Dream. Come. True.

Teenage boys are hardwired with a deep desire to burn things. So to get paid to do it was even better. A brush pile the size of an elephant! I was ecstatic.

I was also clueless. I had never handled a fire outside of a barbecue pit. I knew with a grill you needed some lighter fluid and a match to get the fire going. I figured a similar strategy would apply for a bonfire. So I poured a few gallons of gasoline on the dry wood. Then I sparked up a road flare I'd found in the garage and gently lobbed it toward the stack.

What came next was unexpected.

The blast of flame from the ignition of the gasoline was so substantial that it knocked me off my feet. A second later I discovered I was covered with ash and surrounded by fire. Apparently, the flames were not content to stay contained on the pile. They spread through the surrounding grass and raced along the ground toward the house. We eventually got it out, but not without a few burned fingers, some significantly scorched earth, and a severely stressed-out dad.

Fire can be a lot of fun, but outside of its proper boundaries, it can do serious damage. When contained, fire can be a source of great warmth and life. Box it in with steel and brick in a fireplace and it will bring warmth to your home. Ring it with stones at your camp and its heat will keep you alive. Fire is a gift. But take it outside appropriate boundaries, and it becomes a source of destruction and death. It will destroy you and everything you love.

Sex is the same way. When kept within proper, God-ordained boundaries, it is a gift that will bring warmth and life to a marriage. Take it outside of God's prescribed limits, and it will burn your house down. And right now, around the world, our house is on fire.

As I thought about writing a book on relationships, I knew we had to talk about sex. Some may ask, "Why put it in the dating section?" Because I know people aren't waiting until marriage to start thinking about sex. The book of Proverbs, which was

> **Sex is a gift that will bring warmth and life to a marriage.**

written primarily to an audience of young, single men, addresses the topic of sex in four of the first seven chapters. That's more than 50 percent of those chapters. This makes sense, though, because that's roughly the same percentage of thoughts in a young man's head that are about sex. So if the Bible is opting to discuss sex at that stage in the process, while still single, then so am I. I want to first talk about the presentation of sex in culture today, the effects, and then provide a positive way forward.

A Culture of Sex

We are living in a hyper-sexualized culture. And unlike previous generations, young people today are being raised in it and educated by it. Don't get me wrong, sex has always been popular. That's not new. But the proliferation of sexualized imagery and high-definition pornography—accessible as close as your cell phone—is very new. Think about it: the Internet was not available for widespread public use until the early '90s. In 1993, there were six hundred websites. Total. Now there are billions. In 2004, roughly 45 percent of high school students owned a cell phone.[1] Now 91 percent of high school students get online using mobile devices and most of them are doing so daily.[2] Eighty percent of teenagers check their phones hourly.[3] The iPhone was introduced in 2007, and with it the idea of carrying the worldwide web around with you at all times. That was not that long ago. Now 73 percent of young people report feeling "panicked" if they are ever without their phone.[4] In 2015, CNN reported on a study released by Common Sense Media that found teenagers spend, on average, nine hours a day online.[5] That is more time than they spend sleeping or talking with parents and teachers. Dmitri Christakis, a pediatrician who studies media and children, said, "We are in the midst of a large, uncontrolled experiment on the next generation."[6] Today's young people are truly the first to grow up in a high-speed Internet and image-driven society.

Riding on the waves of all that technology is pornography. The *Huffington Post* reported that porn sites now receive more visitors each month than Netflix, Amazon, and Twitter combined.[7] High-definition videos of sexual acts, often violent, are highly addictive and are typically introduced into adolescents' lives when they are not looking for it and lack sufficient resources to process what they are seeing. We know that in their first exposure to pornography young people are disturbed by the violent images. But they are also fascinated because sex is interesting. It is a confusing experience of being simultaneously repulsed and drawn to this version of sexuality and it lodges deep into young hearts as shame.

The number of young people exposed to porn in their adolescent years is in the high 90-percent range. Mark Regnerus, research professor at the University of Texas, published a book in 2011 entitled *Premarital Sex in America*. In it he interacts with one of the most reliable studies on porn use in eighteen- to twenty-six-year-olds.[8] The survey indicates that 86 percent of young men self-reported interacting with porn at least once a month while 69 percent of young women reported no porn use at all. Now that means 31 percent of young women do use porn. That is one out of every three young women, which is significant. But it is nowhere near the young men, who are about nine out of ten. Just under 50 percent of young men reported viewing pornography weekly.[9]

But while it is mainly men looking at pornography, they are not the only ones affected. Young women are feeling its effects through what Dr. Gail Dines calls "the pornification of young people."[10] She cites an interview in which a pornographer makes the comment: "The girls these days just seem to come to the set porn-ready." She set out to understand what he meant by that.

She discovered the answer in her interview with a convicted child rapist. He explained that in the process of "grooming" a potential victim, perpetrators will tell a young girl that what matters is how hot she is. When she begins to believe that her worth comes from her overt sexuality, he exploits it. Then he dropped this bombshell: "Now the culture does a lot of the grooming for me."

Dr. Dines explained that when young girls watch their pop star role models wear lingerie on stage or in videos or strike overtly sexual poses on magazine covers or in social media posts, it continuously presents these girls with one of two choices: be overtly sexual or be invisible. She asks the question, "What kind of choice is that for a teenage girl when wired into the DNA of an adolescent is the need to be seen?" Thus, increasingly young women feel the pressure to dress, pose, and present themselves in increasingly more sexualized ways. Though they do not watch porn, they are being influenced by a porn culture.

What are the cultural messages? Three simple ideas.

First, sex is casual. It's no big deal. Everybody is doing it. It's just for fun. It's just biology. It's something you do to feel good, like eating a good meal.

Second, sex is essential. It is simultaneously a huge deal, while also somehow being no big deal. So if you are not doing it, that is odd. If you deny it, suppress it, or attempt to control it, you are unhealthy because sex is essential.

And third, sex is primarily physical. Emotions or spirituality need not be a part. View sexual acts online without a single thought about the emotional health of the parties involved. Hook up with strangers at college because you should experiment with one another's bodies without thought of the emotional impact on you or others.

Growing up I heard arguments that maintained when we loosen sexuality from its repressive, religious boundaries we will enter an age of unprecedented enjoyment and freedom. But joy and freedom are not what I have encountered as I have counseled young people throughout the last two decades. Rather, I have found that hypersexualization has hurt us. All of us.

It damages children.

For years the American Psychological Association has raised alarms about the sexualization of young girls. TV shows or music marketed at adolescents increasingly depict sex acts. Pop stars' acts routinely mix symbols of childhood, schoolgirl outfits, or lollipops with sexual imagery.[11] Lingerie is now being marketed to ten- to thirteen-year-old girls. Studies have shown that increasingly this exposure is leading to earlier sexual debuts for young girls and a rise in their issues with weight and body image. Or, for some, sexuality is not only encouraged, it is taken. The results of a nationwide survey conducted by the University of New Hampshire indicate that one in six boys and one in four girls are sexually abused before the age of eighteen.[12] Our thrusting of overt sexuality into the public square has hurt kids.

It divides marriages.

The American Academy of Matrimonial Lawyers reports that 56 percent of their divorce cases involve one party having an obsessive interest in online pornography. The association's president commented, "Eight years ago, pornography played almost no role in divorce in this country."[13]

It disrupts courtship.

One research study among first-year college students discovered that regular use of pornography led young people to presume sexual exclusivity is unrealistic and hold cynical attitudes about love, affection, and marriage.[14] Long hours online has also increased self-reported awkwardness in young men, particularly as they interact with the opposite sex.[15] All are contributing factors to why some are getting married later.

Some have begun to advocate cohabitation as a means of courtship. The belief is that a season of "testing" each other as roommates and sexual partners will lead young people to ultimately find and maintain the right marriage partner. But research overwhelmingly shows how cohabitation actually undermines relationships. Only one in five cohabiting relationships end in marriage. Cohabiting significantly increases the likelihood of divorce.[16] Some have presented serial monogamy as the answer to casual sex with multiple partners. The reality is serial monogamy does not lead to better marriages at all. It simply leads to more unhealthy sex.[17]

Promiscuity also leads to higher rates of depression in women. There is a direct correlation between the number of sexual partners and depression rates in women. Women with two or more sexual partners in their lifetime reveal poorer emotional health than women with zero. Regnerus found that "a sustained pattern of serial monogamy—implying a series of failed relationships—hurts women far more than it hurts men." The common testimony of sexually experienced college women, the researchers say, is a narrative of regret. Indeed, a 2005 study found that young women who had had multiple sex partners were eleven times more likely than virgins to report elevated depressive symptoms.[18]

And the most insidious irony about our culture's obsession with sex: it actually destroys sex!

Psychiatrist and neuroscientist Norman Doidge has explained that sex fires the dopamine system. Dopamine is the "pleasure chemical" in the brain, playing a significant role in reinforcing natural behaviors like eating, drinking, and sex. It is also the same neurotransmitter stimulated by addictive drugs.[19] Anthropologist Helen Fisher has explained that sex releases the hormone oxytocin, which deepens our emotional attachment to another. It is the same hormone released when a mother breastfeeds a baby.

It is designed to bond you. This, she says, is why there is no such thing as "casual sex." Sex is not just a pleasurable physical act. It is designed for bonding.[20] This is the nature of Paul's argument to the Corinthians in 1 Corinthians 6:16 as he explained, "Do you not know that he who is joined to a prostitute becomes one body with her? For, as it is written, 'The two will become one flesh.'" Paul understood that the poetic language found in Genesis 2 about two becoming one depicts an inescapable reality: sexuality is more than the mashing together of bodies; it is the mingling of personhood. This is why breaking up with someone with whom you have had sex can be so difficult. You are, in a very literal sense, going through withdrawal. Do this multiple times and you are, in Paul's words, "sin[ning] against [your] own body" (v. 18). You are hurting yourself, and the research today simply amplifies and explains this warning from centuries ago.

Sex is not just physical. It is a bonding. And herein lies another great modern problem. Many young men are bonding not with a person but with a screen. That intense dopamine rush bathing the brain when a man looks at pornography reinforces the behavior. So men will spend hours online looking for increasingly bizarre and intense sex acts to achieve the same hit. Doidge relates that many of the men he treated had become so dependent on the intensity of extreme explicit imagery to arouse them that they have essentially fried the circuitry so that they are no longer sensitive to normal or slow-building stimuli like romance or dating. And when they do get married, they cannot achieve arousal to have sex with a real person.[21] I thought this might be overblown until recently when I had conversations with five young men who are having trouble with erectile dysfunction because of their addiction to pornography. They have experienced what Paul warned the Ephesians against centuries before, that, "Having lost all sensitivity, they have given themselves over to sensuality"

(Ephesians 4:19 NIV). A constant diet of unrestrained sensuality does not simply give pleasure; it takes away sensitivity. And many young men today are finding that it is robbing them of the sensitivity necessary to be a sexual partner to an actual woman. When the fires of sensuality burn without boundary, they sear our nerve endings. We lose the precious sensitivity needed to enjoy true intimacy with another.

Naomi Wolf, in writing an article for *The New Yorker*, put it succinctly:

> The evidence is in: Greater supply of the stimulant equals diminished capacity. After all, pornography works in the most basic of ways on the brain: It is Pavlovian. An orgasm is one of the biggest reinforcers imaginable. If you associate orgasm with your wife, a kiss, a scent, a body, that is what, over time, will turn you on; if you open your focus to an endless stream of ever-more-transgressive images of cybersex slaves, that is what it will take to turn you on. The ubiquity of sexual images does not free eros but dilutes it.[22]

This is not what young people want. Donna Freitas, research professor at Notre Dame, conducted a ten-year, nationwide research project on sexuality on college campuses. In her interviews, she found that 100 percent of college students said their peers are casual about sex. But 36 percent reported that they felt their peers were too casual about sex. That is one out of every three students who communicated to her that they did not like the dominant cultural narrative about sex.

When she addressed the issue of *hooking up*—meaningless, emotionless sexual encounters—she found even more surprising results. Forty-one percent of young people said hooking up made them feel "profoundly unhappy, disrespected, sad or abused."[23]

The highest praise the other 59 percent could muster was "fine." She found no student who claimed hooking up was awesome or amazing. Just "fine." She reported that students often believe that hookups are their only option. Consequently, there's a lot of suffering, alienation, and shame around hooking up for both men and women, and not living up to hookup culture's expectations of ambivalence and callousness about sex.

But when asked what they want, college students reported to her over and over again that they desire to date. Frequently she heard that "nobody dates here, but I wish they would." "I would go if someone asked me." "I would ask someone if it wasn't so weird."

Dr. Freitas also heard time and again from young people they desired romance. Long hours of talking, dinners, picnics, and trips where they could share their thoughts and desires. She found that young people deeply long for the very thing that hook-up culture denies: emotional connection. Young people want to know and be known.[24] You desire both emotional and physical connection. You desire to be a whole, integrated person. I would submit that you desire this precisely because God designed you this way. Your desires reveal your design.

The Good News

God is not anti-sex. God is actually pro-sex. It was his idea. And he doesn't just simply support sexual activity as a means of baby making. In Proverbs 5:18–19 the Scriptures declare, "Rejoice in the wife of your youth. . . . Let her breasts fill you at all times with delight; be intoxicated always in her love." Just to be clear, a man enjoying a woman's breasts is not a critical component of the reproduction process. God is commanding the husband and wife to not just procreate, but to have fun!

But in that same chapter he warned the young man, "Why

should you be intoxicated, my son, with a forbidden woman and embrace the bosom of an adulteress? . . . The iniquities of the wicked ensnare him, and he is held fast in the cords of his sin. He dies for lack of discipline, and because of his great folly he is led astray" (Proverbs 5:20, 22–23).

God is pro-sex. But like food, God understands there are ways to approach sex that promote health and there are ways that harm health. Sex is also like a fire. Keep it in the fireplace at home, and you have warmth and life. It promotes bonding and oneness with a husband and wife. Take it outside the home, and that same act becomes a force for destruction. The same power that can give life will destroy.

In 1 Thessalonians Paul explained the will of God to a young congregation. So if you have ever asked, "What is God's will for my life?" here is part of it:

> For this is the will of God, your sanctification: that you abstain from sexual immorality; that each one of you know how to control his own body in holiness and honor, not in the passion of lust like the Gentiles who do not know God; that no one transgress and wrong his brother in this matter, because the Lord is an avenger in all these things, as we told you beforehand and solemnly warned you. For God has not called us for impurity, but in holiness. Therefore whoever disregards this, disregards not man but God, who gives his Holy Spirit to you. (4:3–8)

God is not against sex. But he is against its distortion. Why? Because God is pro-people. In 1 Thessalonians 4 Paul called for abstinence from sexual immorality. The reason: that no one transgress or defraud his brother. The word *transgress* means to overstep or cross a boundary, or to enter territory that is not your own. The word *wrong* here means to take what does not belong to you. So how does your participation in lustful activity wrong your brother? If that woman is not your wife, or that man is not your husband, then he or she does not belong to you. That means they belong to someone else. So if you are having sex with them, you are taking something that belongs to a future mate. Their sexuality, their passion, and their body belongs to the one who will promise to love all of them for all of their days. If I am not willing to take on that responsibility, then I have no business trying to take on the benefits of their sexuality. It is crossing a boundary I am not meant to cross. It is attempting to take something that does not belong to me. Ultimately, it is the opposite of love.

A popular argument circling today is, "Shouldn't we explore whether or not we are sexually compatible before we get married?" This, to me, is one of the most asinine arguments I have ever heard. "We have to fool around. How are we going to figure out if we are sexually compatible?" Are you a guy? Is she a girl? Then your parts are going to fit! Much research has been done on this topic. So what do people mean when they say this? What people *really* mean when they advance this argument is that they are concerned about technique. But think about that for a moment. You may ask, "But what if he is a sloppy kisser?" If you are pursuing a man of character, a man who is gentle with you and caring, a man who listens to you, and who promises to love you in sickness and health until death do you part—if you have a man like that, who will lay down his life for you, do you really think he would not be open to some pointers on how to kiss?

More important than physicality: marry someone with character!

Ladies, find someone who is gentle, patient, understanding, and strong, and all of that character will translate into the bedroom. Men, marry a woman who is responsive, tender, patient, and encouraging, and all of that character will translate into the bedroom. If you marry someone with character like that, you two will figure out how to be compatible in the bedroom together. That is what the first year of marriage is for! You marry someone that has godly character, and the two of you will discover how to take care of each other's needs sexually together and it will be fun. I promise! You do not need to figure that out while dating.

In his letters to the Galatians and to the Ephesians, Paul contrasted lustful activity with loving activity. Indeed, they are opposites. Lust, when all is said and done, just wants to use someone for selfish benefit. Love sacrifices for the beloved. They are opposites. So much of what is called "lovemaking" in society today is just an attempt to use another person without having to take on the hassles and inconveniences of genuinely loving them. But in the end, we wound ourselves, our brothers, our sisters, and our society (Galatians 5:19–24; Ephesians 5:1–5).

God wants you to enjoy sex, but within the proper boundaries. He wants us to use it in a way that promotes flourishing for all people and for every part of you. It is not just physical. So save the physical activity for the person who has said to you, "I want your body, your mind, your heart, and a future that lasts until death."

God does not hate sex. He hates the distortion and mismanagement of it. Don't believe the lies. You should be sexual. You should be an adventurous, fun, gentle, sweet, wild, crazy, Olympic gymnast in bed. Have a blast. Just do it with the person you have promised to love forever and has made that same promise to you. That is where your heart, mind, and body are the safest. That is where society is the safest.

I recall walking through the mall once and seeing a giant display of a woman on her hands and knees in the smallest, thinnest lingerie imaginable. She was impossible to miss—the image was plastered ten feet high and twenty feet long across the wall opposite the food court. As I watched families with children, crowds of middle school kids, middle-aged men and women, and the elderly all walk by this massive image, I thought to myself, *One man should see this woman like this. She should be in that pose. She should be making that "come and get me" look. But not in front of these four-year-old kids. Not for these eleven-year-old boys. Not for these middle-aged, married men. She should be dressed like that and looking like that for the man who wants all of her, not just her body.* Sexuality is good. But in the right context. I pray the Lord blesses your sexuality immensely. And I pray you would enjoy it within the boundaries that will bring life to you and the person who said "I do" to all of you—your heart, mind, and body—for years to come.

So What Do We Do?

While there is much more we could say, and maybe should say, about this topic, let me offer two general guidelines for sexuality during our single years. In a hyper-sexualized culture, I believe we must simultaneously become stronger in the right ways and softer in the right ways.

I have observed that many of us today are soft in our barriers against the intrusion of sensual imagery coming into our lives, often through our technology. Because the Internet is accessible anywhere, it has invaded our lives everywhere. We have no boundaries. We are weak in the externals.

Yet, at the same time, I have visited with many young men and women who are very hard on themselves internally. They beat themselves up with guilt over poor relational choices. The deep shame rising from their use of pornography strips them of their vibrancy. A sense of condemnation and hopelessness haunts them. Personally, I get angry at the misuse of sexuality in our culture today because I have watched it steal life and joy from so many young people I care about. Discouragement and disappointment assails them internally.

We must get stronger with external boundaries. In Hebrews 12 the writer said, "In your struggle against sin you have not yet resisted to the point of shedding your blood" (v. 4). He was essentially saying, "You're struggling? You're not even bleeding yet!" We must get tougher here. You need to set limits to the amount of access to the Internet you are engaging in. I have visited many times with young men who feel powerless in the grips of pornography. I ask them when and where they fail. Often it is on their phone late at night. At their most vulnerable moments, when they are tired and in bed, the worldwide web with all of its enticements lay at their bedside. I counsel them to follow Paul's admonition in Romans to, "Make no provision for the flesh, to gratify its desires" (13:14). If access to the Internet while you are alone and tired is an issue, then get your phone out of your bedroom at night.

Your desires reveal your design.

Put all your electronics in a communal room in the house. I have had young men look at me bewildered. One said to me, "But it's my alarm clock." I responded, "Then buy an alarm clock!" Jesus said if your eye causes you to sin to pluck it out (Matthew 5:29)! Now he did not mean that literally, because we could continue to lust with the other eye. But he is expounding a principle: we must be willing to work hard to expel from our lives distorted versions of sexuality. Some of us need to get greater accountability in our lives—regularly checking in with friends who will help us live with integrity. We also need to set boundaries on when and how we will relate to members of the opposite sex. We must get more rigid with ourselves. Not out of some regressive prudishness, but because we want all our sexuality to be channeled toward the person whom we will love, body and soul, forever. For the sake of our marriages, our families, and our own joy, we must get tougher here.

At the same time, this battle against intrusion of illicit sexuality must rise from an internal place, knowing that we are deeply loved. We must be softer with ourselves internally. In that same passage in Hebrews 12, the author said five times that we are sons disciplined by a Father in heaven who loves us. Patrick Carnes, one of the leading voices on sexual addiction, noted that the root of addiction comes from feeling unloved and unlovable.[25]

This same idea is presented in James when he spoke of each of us being tempted when we are lured and enticed by desires that give birth to sin and bring forth death. Then he called us to not be deceived. But notice the nature of the deception. James did not say do not be deceived by the false promises of a particular sin. Rather, he said, "Do not be deceived. . . . Every good gift and every perfect gift is from above, coming down from the Father of lights, with whom there is no variation or shadow due to change" (James 1:16–17). The deception is not about the benefits of a particular act, but about the belief that we have a good Father in heaven who gives good gifts. According to James the lie that launches a million lusts is the belief that God is not a good Father who loves you. Our external controls are useless if we do not deal with this root issue—the deep human desire to be loved. The battle must be fought here first. Addiction is an intimacy disorder.

We must know that our battle against lust is not a battle for acceptance, but a battle from a place of acceptance. We must help one another be softer here. Jesus was gentle with the woman at the well who had a devastated past and present sexual life (John 4).

We must help one another silence the internal voice of condemnation with the compassion of the Father that comes through the grace of the Son and also gives them the power to stand. Empathy dissolves shame. And when we know that we are deeply loved by God and by our community, we can break free from the shackles of shame and move forward with the confidence that we can control our sexuality and not be controlled by it.

Maintaining more controls externally and more compassion internally is fostered by involvement in healthy community. The apostle Paul encouraged his young protégé, Timothy, to "flee youthful passions and pursue righteousness, faith, love, and peace, along with those who call on the Lord from a pure heart" (2 Timothy 2:22). One of God's greatest gifts to us is "us"—a community to belong to. We need elders above us who can model healthy marriages and champion healthy means of courtship. We need churches that can embrace all kinds of people with all manner of struggles, knowing that our kindness leads people to repentance. We need mentors who will help us cast off the shallow, distorted views of sexuality we hear in the culture, and embrace a healthy, life-giving perspective on sex.

For many of us the shame of sexual failure is so strong that we feel powerless to bring the topic up. But we need to. If Paul was unafraid to address sexuality in his correspondence with the Romans, Corinthians, Galatians, Ephesians, Colossians, and Thessalonians, then we should not be reluctant to speak about sexuality with one another. During my first five years in ministry, I watched five men I knew each fall out of ministry due to sexual failure. The common denominator for them all: they were unwilling to risk confessing to others because they were afraid of being spurned or shamed. But James 5:16 says we must confess to one another and pray for one another that we might be *healed*. We need *us*. For me, personally, I have always had a group of men with whom I regularly confess all the temptations and struggles in my life. Whenever those times of confession and prayer are over, I feel safe and I feel strong. I want that for you.

Let me close this chapter by answering the question some of you may be asking: What if I have already failed in this area? What if I have crossed boundaries and engaged in sexuality in a way that is inconsistent with God's design? Am I too far gone? Am I beyond hope? Let me encourage you: do not believe the lie that it is too late. In 1 Corinthians 6:9–11 the apostle Paul stated, "The [sexually immoral] will not inherit the kingdom of God. . . . And such were some of you. But you were washed, you were sanctified, you were justified in the name of the Lord Jesus Christ and by the Spirit of our God."

The Corinthian church was full of people with sexually devastated pasts who found new life and love in a relationship with Christ Jesus. No one comes to God with clean hands. We have all been devastated by sin. Yet God is in the business of washing us and making us new. "There is therefore now no condemnation for those who are in Christ Jesus" (Romans 8:1). Do not believe for a moment you have sinned too much to be loved by God or to be loved by one of his sons or daughters. The same resurrection power that conquered the grave can conquer sexual sin, shame, and addiction. You are never too far gone. The field I lit ablaze with uncontrolled fire many years ago in Beeville, Texas, has regrown. Your misused sexuality need not be the end of the story. The grace of God is far too amazing for an ending like that.

7

a dating case study

isaac receives rebekah // genesis 24

I found love in San Miguel de Allende. In college, a few friends and I jumped on a bus in Nuevo Laredo, rode through the night, and arrived in this little artist colony just north of Mexico City. I remember one evening sitting on the rooftop of La Parroquia, the massive neo-Gothic cathedral that dominates the skyline of the city. From below men in the cavernous sanctuary were singing hymns in Latin that drifted up through the skylight. As the sun set over this colorful city, the combination of sights and sounds flooded my senses with so much beauty it made my heart ache. I remember sitting there next to my buddy Rick and thinking, *Man, I really wish I had a woman here to share this with.* Don't get me wrong, Rick's a good dude, but I wanted a romantic love with a woman I could love until death do us part.

Then I found it. I didn't meet someone special. I wouldn't meet Donna until years later. But it was there on the cobblestoned streets of this sleepy Mexican town that I discovered a little shop off the main road. Inside I found a Gustave Doré lithograph in a thin gold frame with a deep crimson matting. The picture was of a young man helping a beautiful woman off a camel. The man, woman, and camel were all decked out in flowing robes and jewelry. The pageantry of celebration surrounded them, but the focus of the image was the tender moment in the center where the young man held the foot of a woman as he helped her down from the back of the camel. The caption underneath: "Isaac *recibe a* Rebekah." Thankfully, my two years of Spanish class in high school were sufficient to help me translate: "Isaac *receives* Rebekah." I bought the picture and took it home. I was dating no one and had no prospects. But I was struck by the beauty of this union.

Why mention that here? Because while principles can shape our thinking, pictures can capture our imagination. In this chapter I want to show you some of the principles we have discussed, and pick up a few more, as they play out in the divine dance of God bringing together a young couple.

Genesis 24, which illustrates the union of Isaac and Rebekah, is the longest chapter in Genesis. The creation of the world, beginning of humanity, and origin of evil are covered with stunning brevity by Moses. But in chapter 12 the narrative slows down as the rest of the book focuses on a single family. Abraham, the man of faith, believed the promise given to him by God that one day all the nations of the world would be blessed through his offspring. As Abraham neared the end of his life, one challenge remained: finding a wife for his son so that his line could continue. Though the process looks a bit different than our approach today, the narrative nevertheless contains principles that can be applied to our modern context.

Genesis 24:2–3 states, "Abraham said to his servant, the oldest of his household, who had charge of all that he had, 'Put your hand under my thigh, that I may make you swear by the LORD, the God of heaven and God of the earth." Right away, the author wants us to see that something of incredible significance is happening here. Abraham calls not simply for "a" servant, but for his most loyal and proven servant. Even though this is his most reliable man, Abraham makes him swear an oath in the name of God. The servant would know in a heartbeat this is not a normal request. And it's not just any oath. He calls for him to swear while placing his hand under Abraham's thigh. What does this mean? Scholars agree that "under my thigh" is a euphemism that means (ready for this?) *to take a man's sexual organs in your hand.* Wait, what? Why would he do that? The act means one of two things (or possibly both): (1) it is a statement by the oath maker that, if I violate this oath, may your unborn children avenge you against me; or (2) it is an oath that is deeply connected and, thus, accountable to the God who made the covenant with Abraham symbolized by circumcision.

So why are we talking about this? Because it communicates two things to us. First, this oath is about posterity. God promised Abraham that through Isaac would come the descendant of Abraham who would bless the whole world. In order for this to happen, Isaac has to have kids. In order for that to happen, Isaac has to get married. Second, this lets us know that God takes marriage very seriously. Let this be an encouragement to you. God cares about your love life. He cares about who you marry. You are not alone as you deal with your desire to be married. God is invested in your life and he cares about families. In fact, in Ephesians 3 he is called the God from whom every family on earth is named. The act of naming in this context carries the idea of bringing into existence. God loves to create families. Sometimes when we think about our love life we can feel very alone. But you are not alone. God cares. This is a serious issue to him.

Specifically, *who* you marry is incredibly serious. We see this in the oath Abraham makes his servant swear to:

> That you will not take a wife for my son from the daughters of
> the Canaanites, among whom I dwell, but will go to my country
> and to my kindred, and take a wife for my son Isaac. (Genesis
> 24:3–4)

What's going on here? Is Abraham a racist? No. This is not about race, it's about faith. The Canaanites believed in multiple gods. Much of their worship of these gods centered around violence and sensual, sexual activity. This stood at odds with Abraham's relationship with God. Though his family back in the old country was not perfect, they retained an allegiance to God. Thus, as Abraham considered his duty of finding a spouse for his son, his first and, really, only criteria is that she must be a believer in the one true God. Abraham's servant will travel more than five hundred miles to find a wife like this for Isaac! What does this amazing fact teach you? If no one in your present social circle is passionate about the things of God, then get out there and meet some more people! Don't settle.

Notice as the story unfolds that a believer alone will not do. The servant responds to Abraham with a question:

> The servant said to him, "Perhaps the woman may not be will-
> ing to follow me to this land. Must I then take your son back to
> the land from which you came?" (v. 5)

This seems like a reasonable question. If she is unwilling to make the trip, should your son resettle back in the old country? He can move near her family, let her continue her career, and so forth. But this request elicits a strong reaction from Abraham.

> Abraham said to him, "See to it that you do not take my son
> back there." (v. 6)

Why is Abraham so emphatic about this? He explains:

The LORD, the God of heaven, who took me from my father's house and from the land of my kindred, and who spoke to me and swore to me, "To your offspring I will give this land," he will send his angel before you, and you shall take a wife for my son from there. (v. 7)

Abraham's concern reveals an important point: marry someone who is walking by faith.

What kind of woman would be unwilling to move? You might say, "A prudent one. She doesn't even know these people!" But you've got to understand that this is not a complete stranger. This is family. And this would be a good arrangement that fit in line with the customs of arranged marriage of the day. So the kind of woman who would be unwilling to come back would be one who was unwilling to exercise the kind of radical faith that guided the life of Abraham and Isaac. Abraham willingly left all the comforts of home and his life in that

> **Trust that the God who saved you can provide a mate for you.**

part of the world in absolute faith in the promises of God. He and his son had been living radically by faith their whole lives. So when it came time for Isaac to get married, he needed a wife willing to walk boldly by faith as well. If she's trying to negotiate, then she's not the right one.

This is the kind of marriage you want—someone who wants to pursue the Lord with the same intensity that you do. If he or she is not willing to live by faith with the same passion you are, then you do not want to run together for the rest of your lives.

As soon as I say that, I know some of you may be thinking, *That's easy for you to say, Ben. But what are the odds I'm going to find someone like that? It seems like all the good ones are gone.* But I challenge you to adopt Abraham's perspective: the God who leads us will also provide for us. Abraham is a man of faith. This leads me to my next point: trust that the God who saved you can provide a mate for you.

Many of us can trust God with a lot of stuff, but when it comes to marriage we're scared to death he's going to do something terrible to us: we'll never meet someone, or if we trust God to provide a husband we will have to wait forever and then the guy will be weird or not at all what we want. So we take it into our own hands, which usually involves trying to dress a certain way, or act a certain way, or say certain things in order to "catch," "land," "bag," or "win" our mate. As a result, trusting the Lord (with the side effects of joy, peace, and a whole lot more) goes flying out of our lives. Don't be a *believer* who doesn't believe God will care for you. If you have trusted God with your eternal destiny, you can trust him with your love life.

Look at Abraham's final words to his servant:

> But if the woman is not willing to follow you, then you will be free from this oath of mine; only you must not take my son back there. (v. 8)

Note the perspective: Abraham is willing to let it go. If seeking marriage and living for God become at odds, he chooses God. Translation: I'd rather be single than marry second-best.

The story continues:

> So the servant put his hand under the thigh of Abraham his
> master and swore to him concerning this matter. Then the
> servant took ten of his master's camels and departed, taking all
> sorts of choice gifts from his master; and he arose and went to
> Mesopotamia to the city of Nahor. (vv. 9–10)

The servant begins the journey and as he arrives in the home country, we can read how he engages in a strategy to fulfill his oath and learn several tips along the way to apply to the pursuit of marriage.

Go to the Right Place

Notice in verse 10 the servant travels until he arrives to the city of Nahor. This is not the name of the city; Nahor is actually Abraham's brother. This seems intuitive. If I am looking for a relative of my master, let me go where his relatives live. Though this seems like an obvious point, I have been amazed recently by how many believers in Christ do not follow this simple strategy. Recently, speaking to a group of singles in Dallas, I was stunned by how many young believers were attending church for their spiritual growth, yet were relying solely on the bar scene and dating apps to meet someone. Are there some great guys at the bar or on Tinder? I am sure there are. Yet, you have diluted the pool significantly. Your probability of finding someone who is passionately pursuing the things of God just went way down. Ladies, let's say you want to marry a man after God's own heart. Maybe out of one hundred single guys at your church, ninety are total goobers. But that still gives you one in every ten who is the kind of man you'd want your son to be like! What are your odds on Tinder? At any given bar? One in one hundred? One thousand? I'm not saying you can't meet a good person in those places; I'm just saying you've likely made your search much harder by introducing into the mix a lot more people who would not be good options. If I'm looking for a Texan, for example, I can probably find one in Utah if I search long enough. But my job is way easier if I search in TEXAS! In the same way, you can find a solid believer on Tinder, but you're far more likely to find one if you are involved in Christ-exalting churches or ministries in your city. So get involved in those places.

Go Where the Workers Are

Furthermore, notice how Abraham's servant doesn't just arrive to the right city; he gets more specific than that:

> He made the camels kneel down outside the city by the well of water at the time of evening, the time when women go out to draw water. (v. 11)

Notice what kind of women: those who are working. That's important! All throughout the Bible godly women have been those who are willing to work hard. We will see it here in a moment with Rebekah. Moses' wife was a shepherdess. The Shulammite in Song of Solomon worked in the vineyard. Ruth gleaned in the fields. A woman who is willing to work is a prize. In Proverbs 31 the ideal wife is described as one who "girds herself with strength and makes her arms strong" (v. 17 NASB).

Why is this valuable? Continue reading Proverbs 31. The woman of great worth is not a passive woman. She feeds and clothes her family, conducts wise business transactions, deals successfully in real estate, invests, and serves among the needy.

She gets stuff done. And what she accomplishes improves the lives of everyone around her. You want to be around a woman like that! When I was single, I used to pray that I would meet my wife-to-be on the mission field. I wanted to meet her while she was doing the work of ministry. When I met Donna she was working hard for her church, far beyond what her job description outlined. She paid for college by working for a barbecue restaurant. She had calloused hands. That's what I'm talking about!

Let me apply this in two ways. First, you want an industrious person. A lazy person will frustrate you to no end when you need to pay bills, earn an income, clean your home, and raise your children. He or she will be a weight you must carry rather than an additional engine to propel your life and ministry forward. Ladies, take your cues from Rebekah. She knew what it was to work hard. And take note of Isaac. His servant comes rolling in with ten camels and some gold. That means that Isaac had some money! Your man does not need to be rich, but he does need to be employed. Make sure you marry a guy who understands what it is to earn a paycheck and provide.

Second, you are going to find workers working. So if you are only going to social gatherings to meet people, you may not meet this person. Gentlemen, if you want to find a girl like this, she is probably not just sitting out there somewhere in the church. She's probably on a serve team. Ladies, this kind of man is probably out there working with the ministries that are making a difference in your city. You want a good one? Go to the well. Go where they'd be working hard at the things that matter.

Surrender the Search

Notice the first thing the servant does upon reaching his destination:

> He said, "O LORD, God of my master Abraham, please grant me
> success today and show steadfast love to my master Abraham."
> (Genesis 24:12)

He prays! This is important: actively invite God into the process! In 1 Peter 5:7 we are called to cast *all* our anxiety upon him. Why? Because Peter said, "He cares for you." What you are thinking and what you are feeling matter to God. There is nothing too small. Like a caring mom or dad, God wants to hear from his kids. Do not be too shy to invite God into this process.

Look for a Gracious Person

In Genesis 24:14 we get the substance of the servant's prayer:

> Let the young woman to whom I shall say, "Please let down your
> jar that I may drink," and who shall say, "Drink, and I will water
> your camels"—let her be the one whom you have appointed for
> your servant Isaac. By this I shall know that you have shown
> steadfast love to my master."

Now, I cannot affirm that it will always work out like this. *Lord, let the person I sit by at the coffee shop today be my future spouse.* However, I do think it is significant to see what manner of activity he hopes to find the woman engaged in. Not only would she be hard-working, but she would be gracious. Her hospitality extends beyond merely answering his request for a drink. In fact, it extends far beyond simply meeting his minimum requirement. Camels can drink up to twenty-five gallons of water, and this dude had one hundred of them. So this is a serious test! He is looking for a woman who is extravagantly hospitable, even to strangers.

Being gracious is very attractive. Proverbs 11:16 says, "A gracious woman attains honor" (NASB). I have certainly seen this to be true. In college, I had two friends of the opposite sex who were pretty, but not necessarily known as the most physically attractive girls in the school. However, both of these young ladies were extraordinarily kind to everyone. They were encouragers. I watched as these two girls were asked out by different guys all the time. Constantly! Why? Because kindness is attractive and graciousness is a beautiful quality. First Peter 3:3–4 says, "Do not let your adorning be external—the braiding of hair and the putting on of gold jewelry, or the clothing you wear—but let your adorning be the hidden person of the heart with the imperishable beauty of a gentle and quiet spirit, which in God's sight is very precious." Peter was not telling women to avoid getting dressed up. Rather, he was saying that your character will take you farther than your cosmetics. Cultivate the beauty of a gracious disposition above anything else.

Guys, we are meant to do the same. Proverbs 19:22 states, "What is desirable in a man is his kindness" (NASB). In high school I had a Bible study leader who was, let's just say, homely. But he had a gorgeous wife. I worked up the courage to ask him how on earth he pulled that off. He was not offended by the question in the slightest. He then recounted the story of the day he worked up the nerve to ask her out on a first date and she said yes. He recalled how when he went home he was a nervous wreck. He paced the room, praying, *O God, what am I going to do when I am sitting across the table looking at this woman? What on earth could I possibly have to offer?* He then threw his Bible open and read the passage above—assuring him that what is desirable about a man is kindness. He got down on his knees and made a vow to God that very moment: *Lord, no matter what happens, I will be kind.* Fast-forward a few years and they're married. One night, while lying in bed together, he asked her, "How did I pull this off?" She answered, "I just remembered you were so kind." He quietly nodded to the heavens. *Good one, Lord.* Grace is attractive. Don't leave home without it.

The story of Isaac and Rebekah also highlights God's graciousness.

> Before he had finished speaking, behold, Rebekah who was born to Bethuel the son of Milcah, the wife of Abraham's brother Nahor, came out with her jar on her shoulder. The girl was very beautiful, a virgin, and no man had had relations with her; and she went down to the spring and filled her jar and came up. (Genesis 24:15–16 NASB)

The Lord chooses to be gracious to Abraham's servant. Before his prayer is even over, a relative is on the way! Now before you roll your eyes at how easy it was for him to find Isaac a girl, I invite you to keep in mind that Isaac is forty at this point in time. Before it was "easy," Isaac had to wait for a few decades! But God's timing is perfect. And we get the sense that God is ready to move things along in this area of Isaac's life.

Though the servant does not know yet, we discover that Rebekah is indeed a relative of Abraham. She fits the criteria. The text also describes her as beautiful.

Find someone whose character makes you want to fall on your knees and thank God.

Bonus! That was not part of Abraham's request or the servant's prayer. Yet it is definitely a plus. The text also notes that she is a virgin. This is also meant to be a compliment. She has kept herself sexually pure. The Bible does celebrate this.

However, I also want you to notice that sexual purity was not part of Abraham's criteria for a wife for Isaac. It was not part of Abraham's criteria because it is not part of God's criteria. In the lineage of Jesus, several men and women will appear who had sexual histories that deviated far from God's design, including Judah, Rahab, David, and Bathsheba. God has blessed and used mightily men and women whose sexual backgrounds were not pristine. So take heart. Our God is a God of forgiveness and mercy who loves to restore. The bride of Jesus himself, the church, did not come to the altar pure. But God delights in redemption stories. Do not lose hope. Virginity was not a prerequisite for God's acceptance of his bride. It will not be in the criteria of a godly spouse either. Yet there is great honor in purity. So even if you have had a checkered past, you can, and should, start fresh today.

Back to our story. All the servant knows now is that this girl is attractive and carrying a water jug. Sometimes attractiveness is an okay place to start! So he moves toward her and initiates.

Then the servant ran to meet her and said, "Please give me a little water to drink from your jar." (v. 17)

Now watch her response:

She said, "Drink, my lord." (v. 18)

She is respectful. As a younger person addressing an older one, she refers to him with a title of dignity.

> And she *quickly* let down her jar upon her hand and gave him a
> drink. (v. 18, emphasis added)

She responds positively to his request for a drink. The author notes that she does so "quickly." She doesn't roll her eyes and begrudgingly fulfill his request. She is quick to serve.

> When she had finished giving him a drink, she said, "I will draw
> water for your camels also, until they have finished drinking. So
> she *quickly* emptied her jar into the trough and ran again to the
> well to draw water, and she drew for all his camels. (vv. 19–20,
> emphasis added)

Not only does she water the camels, but she also does this "quickly"—even *running* to get to them all.

Watch and Learn

As Rebekah begins to act, note the servant's response:

> The man gazed at her in silence to learn whether the LORD had
> prospered his journey or not. (v. 21)

What does he do? He *watches*.

It's one thing to hear what someone has to say. It is an entirely different thing to watch how they live. Here we see one of the great benefits of the servant searching for the girl rather than Isaac. If an attractive young man rolled up with nice jewelry and some camels, there might have been a bunch of girls from the town suddenly interested in fetching water. Isaac may have run into the problem a lot of wealthy and famous people do: wondering if the person who is interested in them actually cares about them as a person, or just their money. The servant does not have to wonder. He watches Rebekah help an aging man and some camels. Why? Because she is a good woman. Now, you may not be able to send an employee to do some relational scouting for you, but you can copy the servant's strategy. Watch someone's life.

I remember walking into the lunchroom in college and watching as a young guy did his best to try to get a date with a friend of mine. As he knelt at the table, I heard him continue to throw lines at her, trying to convince her to get in the car with him. He seemed slick, as though this wasn't his first rodeo. And yet she continually turned him down. At one point I overheard him protest, "How will you ever get to know me if you don't go out with me?" She responded, "Sorry, it's not going to happen." Finally, after he realized his cause was lost, he left. As an older brother whose sister was about to begin college, I was fascinated. I had seen many of my female friends go on dates their freshman year against their better judgment because of a guy's persistence. They all had stories of being mid-date and realizing that not only were they not interested in the guy, they did not feel safe. I wanted my sister to have the confidence to turn guys like that down. So when I saw my friend Libby exude that confidence, I had to learn her secret. I approached and asked her, "How did you do that? From whence came the inner strength to shut down his advances?" She explained, "Ben, the community of people seeking Jesus at our college is small. In four years I have never seen him anywhere serving. And no one I know has ever seen him involved in what God is doing on this campus. So I am not going to waste my time." It seemed so simple, yet so profound. Anybody can be charming for an hour on a first date. Who knows if he's really a good guy or not? She decided that you don't even get a shot one-on-one with her unless she's been able to see or hear of you serving and caring for others. I called my sister right away to pass along the wisdom I had just received. My sister has since gone on to marry very well and I take all the credit for that decision.

Worship Worthy

The servant watches Rebekah react to an unexpected situation with the utmost poise and grace. When he sees this character displayed, he feels the freedom to engage in a discussion about commitment.

> When the camels had finished drinking, the man . . . said, "Please tell me whose daughter you are. Is there room in your father's house for us to spend the night?" She said to him, "I am the daughter of Bethuel the son of Milcah, whom she bore to Nahor." She added, "We have plenty of both straw and fodder, and room to spend the night." (vv. 22–25)

He discovers that not only is she continually hospitable, but she is indeed related to Abraham. As it dawns on him that she is a member of the family of God and exhibits the character of a child of God, he does the most natural thing.

> The man bowed his head and worshiped the LORD and said, "Blessed be the LORD, the God of my master Abraham, who has not forsaken his steadfast love and his faithfulness toward my master. As for me, the LORD has led me in the way to the house of my master's kinsmen." (vv. 26–27)

He worships! Ladies and gentlemen, let me beg you, do not pull out the ring until you find someone whose character makes you want to fall on your knees and thank God. I remember a conversation in college a group of us guys had as we were encouraging a friend to work up the courage to ask out the girl he was interested in. He told us, "I just feel so unworthy. This is how I feel . . ." He then struck a pose like he was up to bat at a baseball game. He called out in an announcer's voice, "Now batting out of his league . . . Jenks Currie." We all laughed. But then one of our friends spoke up and said, "Jenks, that's exactly what you want! You don't want to end up with a girl to whom you could say, 'Y'know, you were about the best I could pull off.' You want a relationship story where you could look into the face of that person and say, 'Only God could have done this.'" You want a relationship that inspires worship.

Look for Someone Who Is Ready to Live by Faith

Then Rebekah did what you would expect any girl to do:

> Then the young woman ran and told her mother's household about these things. (v. 28)

In the verses that follow, the servant recounts the story to her family. When her brother, who was serving as the head of the household, sees the money, he tries to get the servant to stick around for what was understood in the culture to be an indiscriminate amount of time. Later in Genesis we find that her brother is a pretty shifty guy, cheating his relatives out of proper wages for a year's worth of labor. But here the servant is undaunted. He insists they leave promptly. Reaching an impasse, her brother defers to Rebekah for the decision. This propels us to the climactic moment. She is asked directly: Will you go?

> They said, "Let us call the young woman and ask her."
>
> And they called Rebekah and said to her, "Will you go with this man?" She said, "I will go." So they sent away Rebekah their sister and her nurse, and Abraham's servant and his men. (vv. 57–59)

If you have to wait until you are forty, then wait. It is better to get the ideal person with bad timing than to get married at your ideal timing to the wrong person. The people of God do not have to compromise their convictions to find love.

Strive for the Blessing of the Family

You see another tip unfold in verses 60–61:

> They blessed Rebekah and said to her, "Our sister, may you become thousands of ten thousands, and may your offspring possess the gate of those who hate him!" Then Rebekah and her young women arose and rode on the camels and followed the man. Thus the servant took Rebekah and went his way.

Even if you do not have a great family situation, sometimes marriages can be catalytic for healing.

Even if your family has ideas you do not necessarily agree with, it is still valuable to seek their input. If parents are resistant to a union, and you are patient enough to listen to their feedback, often you will find wisdom in their concerns. Approaching marriage tends to surface issues in a family that can be deeply divisive and hurtful, or unifying and helpful. Though Rebekah's family is not completely honest (as we discover in later chapters of Genesis), they are won over by patient persistence—enough to issue a beautiful blessing! Involving family in the romantic process, though frustrating at times, can often result in growth and blessing for all if we are patient with the process.

Not only can the courtship of a man and a woman be a blessing to each other's families, but it can be an enormous blessing to the world as well. In Ephesians 5 we learn that God ordained that the marriage of a man and a woman serve as a living picture to the world of Christ's union with his people. The story of Isaac and Rebekah provides just that. The Father sends a servant to find a chosen bride. When the servant locates her, he tells her that all of the riches of the father have been given to the son. She is invited to make a decision: Will you take a journey by faith, trusting that the son will take you to be in his father's house forever? This is our story as believers as well! God the Father has declared to the world that his Son, Jesus Christ, has come to be the caring husband of his bride, the church. All who will trust in him are welcomed into the Father's house forever.

This is one of the greatest blessings of successful dating. As we date one another with faith, honesty, and kindness, we can enjoy a healthy process of finding a husband or wife while also displaying to the world the wonderful way Jesus Christ has loved us.

engaged: union

The brief season of engagement exists to allow
a young couple to focus on the complexities
of bringing their two lives together as one. It
is not simply a time to work on the wedding,
but rather a time to work on the marriage.
Engagement, in its essence, is about union.

8

how to know
that you know

I was supposed to be studying Greek. The library was filled with anxious seminary students furiously cramming for our upcoming final exams. But as I sat at my desk surrounded by books in a foreign language, I was researching wedding rings. Analyzing the cut, clarity, and carat of various diamonds, trying to figure out what I could afford. I was also sneaking into the break room to periodically work the phones to get the best price from dealers across the country. How long does it take to make a ring? Six months? A year? I pulled a calendar out to try to figure out how long I would have to wait until I could cash out of singleness forever and marry Donna.

"Two days." What? The man on the other line repeated the sentence. "Two days. I could get you the ring you want in two days." I felt numb all over my body. I assumed I would have to wait six months for the ring, then another six months for the engagement. I was trying to figure out how I was going to survive another full year of waiting to be married. Now I realized I could get engaged in days, not months. Hours even! We could be married in six months. Maybe even four!

A warm feeling crept through my entire body. *This is it, Ben. You could be ready to end singleness, forever. You could be stepping into marriage, forever. Are you ready?* I remember hearing the response arise from my heart: *Absolutely. Let's do this.*

But how did I get to this point? How did I know Donna was "the one" I wanted to spend the rest of my life with?

How will you know?

Maybe you are standing on the edge of a relationship that has lasted several months, or even years. You are an age where you could get married. You have the finances to afford it. You love each other. You can imagine a future together.

But how do you know when you are ready to cross the threshold; that you have found the right one? What are the clues that lead us to conclude that a relationship is ready for commitment? What are the evidences that prove that a couple is ready for engagement? In this chapter I will offer you four realities that, when all four are present in a relationship, can give you the confidence to know that you know you're with the right one.

Four Ways to Know That You Know

A Strong Sense of Commitment

First, you must discover within yourself and the other person a strong sense of mutual commitment to the relationship. You need to observe in you both a resolve to stay with each other even when it is hard. Another way to say it would be to ask you this question: Do you *want* to work through problems? I am not asking if you are *able* to work through problems. I bet you possess the ability to grit your teeth and endure all manner of challenges. But you don't want a marriage like that. I am asking if you *want* to resolve problems with this person. That is one of the ways that you know you have found the person you want to be with. In Song of Solomon, the book of romantic love in the Bible, the beloved said to her man, "Set me as a seal upon your heart, as a seal upon your arm, for love is strong as death, jealousy is fierce as the grave. Its flashes are flashes of fire, the very flame of the LORD" (8:6). How is love like death? They are alike in their strength. When death takes hold of something, it never lets go. Love is like this. How do you know real love? It grabs hold and says, "I am staying for better and for worse." There is a deep sense of commitment. A resolve to stay even when it requires the discomfort of working through problems.

I'm not asking if you would miss them if they were gone. I am not asking if you like having them around. All that can be true with someone who is nice, sweet, cool, attractive, and not the one for you. But I have found that many people who are dating great people who aren't a great fit, kinda already know it's not the right person. And as soon as difficulty arises, the first voice that speaks in their mind says, *I know this relationship is not right.*

When you are first attracted to someone, it is akin to striking a match. *Whoosh!* There is a rush of excitement. *Wow! That person is cute!* It is an intoxicating feeling. There is suddenly a flame where once there was none. Romance is like this. It ignites something in you. Suddenly you feel like singing and dancing. The birds are singing. Food tastes better. All is wonderful. At this point, many people make the mistake of introducing sexual contact into the relationship. This is like spraying lighter fluid on that match. The flame keeps going. It even spreads! But there is no depth. There are no coals or deep embers to keep the fire going through cold nights or rainy seasons. So if you jump into marriage with a match-and-lighter-fluid kind of relationship, you will wake up a few years in and ask yourself, *Do I even like this person?*

I promise you, you want to know the answer to that question before the wedding.

What you need in the moments of difficulty and disappointment in marriage are deep coals—glowing white-hot embers of commitment that will continue to burn even as the rain falls and that can be kindled afresh into a blaze again and again throughout your life. How do you know you have

> **Evaluate long enough to see how the relationship survives when drama comes.**

that kind of deep resolve in your relationship? Well, as you date, grow closer, and evaluate each other, over time you will see how you both navigate the two great tests of a relationship: temptation and trials. You've got to evaluate long enough to see how the relationship survives when drama comes.

Think about how they select Navy SEALs. The men who make it through the screening process to go to BUD/S—the grueling training program you must go through to become a SEAL—are certified physically fit enough to handle all the rigors of the program. Yet there is still a 75 percent dropout rate. Why? Because over the course of several months, they dunk these men in freezing cold water again, and again, and again. Then they make them charge out of the icy ocean, roll around in the sand on the beach, and when they are encrusted with sand from head to toe, run down the beach for miles. Next, they dive back into that icy ocean and do it all over again. And again. And again. This process will most likely not kill them. Yet, at some point, some of the men begin to evaluate, *How bad do I really want this job?* Their bodies can handle the strain, without question. But over time, the difficulties test their resolve. The pain and discomfort continually raises the question in their minds of whether they *want* to keep doing this to themselves. They liked the idea of being a SEAL, but the reality of being a SEAL is way too much of a hassle. All throughout this time, instructors will periodically offer the men a warm blanket. A Snickers bar. A ride in the car. Temptations. All they have to do is quit. For many, when the trials are sufficiently bad and the temptations sufficiently good, they rise up, walk out, ring a bell three times, and are out of BUD/S. The trials and the temptations serve to expose what is in your heart: how badly you want to be a part of this team. It is the same with marriage.

Song of Solomon says it this way: "Many waters cannot quench love, neither can floods drown it. If a man offered for love all the wealth of his house, he would be utterly despised" (8:7). How do you know the commitment is there for you? It overcomes hardships. No waters can quench it. So wait and see. Date long enough to experience some arguments about fundamental issues. Wait for that situation where you begin to see a little character flaw or an annoying habit in the other that you realize will never go away. Then watch yourself. Does it make you want to quit? Does it make you long for someone else? Or if some temptation comes your way, true love will despise the offer of enticement. It cannot be bought. So wait and see. Can your relationship survive temptation? Watch and see when one of her ex-boyfriends or one of his ex-girlfriends comes to town. Watch what they do. If someone you've always thought was cute shows some interest in you, what will you do? How do you know you've got the right one? Because you see within yourself and within the other person a commitment to stay that no trial and no temptation can dislodge.

I was the last one of my close friends to get married. Every single one of my groomsmen at my wedding was married. So, of course, as I dated I got advice from them about "how you know when you know." And they often said, "You'll just know." Which, as you might know if any of your friends have ever said that to you, is supremely unhelpful. So I decided to press one of them on what exactly he meant when he said that.

"Does that mean you and your wife never fought when you were dating?"

"No, we definitely had some disagreements," he responded.

"Then what exactly was 'easy' about this dating relationship as opposed to others?" I pressed.

He explained, "In previous relationships, when it got hard, there was always a nagging question of whether this was the right thing. Should this work? Should we be doing this?" He continued, "But with the right person, we would disagree, and it would be hard sometimes, but when I looked within I found a deep resolve that kept reinforcing the stance of my heart: *I am not going anywhere. I want this to work.* And I saw in her a similar resolve. That resolve must be present in both of you. We both believed that this relationship was worth navigating through the pain to come to resolution and deeper intimacy. I didn't care if an old girlfriend came back around. There were no other fish in the sea for me. No temptation or trial, no suffering or seduction, could get me to leave. I only wanted her." That kind of resolve takes time to build and time to discover.

For some of you it will not only take some time to discover that kind of commitment, it will take some distance too. It did for me. As Donna and I dated longer, the prospect of marriage became more and more of a possibility. And as I looked within, I just wasn't sure how I felt. I know that sounds terrible, but I was conflicted. I had some fear about commitment. Now I know some of you may be shocked to hear that. *A guy with commitment issues? What do you mean?* Just take it by faith. There was one, and I was him.

We were approaching a summer when her band was leading worship all over the country. Meanwhile, I was looking to head off to seminary and was unsure about whether or not our lives were going to lead us in very different directions. So I asked her if we could not talk at all on the phone that summer. All the constant input of talking to her every day made it hard for me to evaluate. We agreed that we could write letters. (By this I mean the following: we took out pieces of paper and wrote words to each other and put that piece of paper in a mailbox, and then the mailman came and picked it up and passed that same piece of paper to the other person several days later. You've maybe seen something like this in old movies.) This slowed down the pace of communication considerably and bought me some time to think. I remember, a few months later, I was on a friend's boat on the Fourth of July. As I watched the fireworks shimmer down into the water around us, I struggled to understand what this feeling was deep inside of me. I remember thinking, *I think I'm sad.* Then I asked myself, *Why? Why are you downcast, o my soul?* It was that moment I realized I missed Donna. That was a weird experience for me. I questioned it. *What does this mean?* I sensed within, *What it means, dum-dum, is that I would rather live life with her than without her. It means I want to be with her no matter what hardship it brings.* I remember reasoning, *I think this might mean that I love her.* Now, if some of you are marveling at the thickheadedness of this internal dialogue, let me respond by pointing out the following: you may not know guys very well. For many men, they find themselves a bit sealed off from their emotions at times. What I have found is that for these men, what worked for me works for them. Distance and time are great friends when trying to discern if commitment is present.

Does this mean that you will always feel a strong sense of passion? No. What I am about to write here will sound very unromantic, but it is reality. You will be playing the percentages. What

I mean is this: if 90 percent of the time you feel confident they are the one for you, that is a good sign. Our emotions rise and fall throughout the day. No one has a single, sustained emotional experience every minute of every day. That means there will be moments you feel indifferent about the love of your life. That means there will be moments when you feel as though you could do fine without him or her. My question is, how many moments of the day are filled with thoughts like that? If 90 percent of the time you feel confident he or she is the one, then that means 10 percent of the time you will have some doubt. That would be a good percentage balance. That might be as certain as you get to be in life. Now if four or five out of every ten thoughts about him or her are, *Eh, I don't know if this is going to work*, then don't get married! Even a fifty-fifty chance that you think it will work is bad odds. Wait long enough in dating to see if resolve becomes evident.

When you get married, you will sign a document that declares to God and the world, "I am binding myself to this person for the rest of my life." Make sure that piece of paper is a reflection of what you feel inside. True love is stronger than death, more powerful than the grave. Wait long enough to make sure that conviction is present.

A Growing Skill of Communication

Beyond commitment you must also add the skill of communication. You need more than just a resolve to stick this thing out. You must both develop the ability to communicate. Can you navigate relational conflict? Can you disagree in a way that promotes unity, rather than disunity? Proverbs 12 says it this way:

> There is one whose rash words are like sword thrusts, but the tongue of the wise brings healing. (v. 18)

When you disagree, do your words become weapons? Do you go into attack mode? Are you willing to wound the other person so you can win the argument? Or, even when your feelings are hurt, are you able to speak words to each other that are wise and bring healing and health to the relationship? You need the skill of communication for marriage to work.

You can be crazy about a person, but if the two of you cannot communicate when life gets hard, you are not going to make it. Let me give you a preview of engagement. After the magical moment when you produce and/or receive a ring, you immediately plunge into planning a massive event for everyone you know. Do you think this is going to create some stress? It will. And you are going to want to possess the ability to communicate with each other to be able to make numerous decisions over the next several months. You must be able to talk.

It makes me nervous when I counsel a couple who says they never disagree. Let me be clear: I don't think you should be fighting all through courtship. I also do not think you should ever raise your voice or yell at each other. But if you never disagree about issues, then you may not know each other well. No two human beings are going to line up perfectly on every conceivable issue. So if you are truly using the dating season to evaluate and get to know each other, issues *will* come up that cause disagreement. Can you work through those in a healthy way? Or does one of you dominate the conversation and the other one hide your feelings? Are either of you refusing to share what you really think? Or do you both explode and attack?

Proverbs 15 says, "A gentle tongue is a tree of life, but perverseness in it breaks the spirit" (v. 4). What happens when your feelings are hurt? Do you lash out in anger, attempting to break the other's will? Do you freeze the other out with the silent treatment—waiting him or her out until he or she breaks and apologizes? Or can you speak to each other in a gentle way that is a tree of life for the both of you, producing growth and intimacy? Which is it going to be?

Let me try to help here. When you disagree with someone, you need to focus on his or her *actions* and your *feelings*. Do not try to guess the other person's motives. That's too low-percentage of a shot. So statements like "you're trying to humiliate me" or "you're trying to make me look dumb" are not constructive. You have no idea what the other is trying to do. You don't know the motives. Focus your disagreements on actions and your own feelings.

For example, early in our marriage I remember Donna and I were at a party talking with some people. She commented on something personal about me that elicited a laugh from the crowd. As soon as that happened, I shut down. I did not like that. It frustrated me so much that we had to talk about it later. What is a constructive way to handle that? To focus on her actions and my feelings. So how should I respond in this scenario? I should say, "Hey, when you made a joke at my expense in front of those people [her action], it made me feel humiliated. It made me feel small. It also made me feel like you are not on my side, or that you are willing to hurt me if it seems opportune for you. I don't want to feel that way." It is hard to talk like this, especially for men. It feels weak to say, "My feelings got hurt." It feels so much more natural to respond, "Why are you trying to make me look dumb? Why are you so obsessed with being cool that you will throw me under the bus at any chance?" But that is not helpful. It assumes her motive. It is an accusation that her internal drive is her ambition and your destruction. That may not be the case at all. It may have been something she thought you'd both find funny. Or it may have come out in a moment of insecurity because she was not feeling confident that night. You do not know for certain. But by attacking her motive, you put her on the defensive and you significantly complicate any efforts to reach mutual understanding and deeper unity.

When speaking about healthy community to the Ephesians, Paul exhorted them, "Speaking the truth in love, we are to grow up in every way" (4:15). This is healthy communication. From a place of love, I speak the truth. What are the true things you can know? All you can know are their actions and your feelings. Anything else is conjecture and assumption. So when you are hurt, try to first focus on their actions: "Hey, do you remember when you made that joke about me having a big head?" Then focus on your emotions:

> ## Distance and time are great friends when trying to discern if commitment is present.

"That made me feel embarrassed and it made me feel like we were not a team in that moment. And I really like feeling like we are a team." This gives them the room to respond by saying, "I don't want to ever make you feel embarrassed. That's never my goal. I don't want you to ever feel like I am not on your team either. Because I am. What do I need to do differently?" This is your opportunity to communication your need: "Please don't mock me in front of people. I don't like it." Wow. Problem solved! When Donna and I had our moment of disagreement after the party, our conversation finally arrived at a place like this.

This conversation also gave Donna the opportunity to respond, "When you tell me how I've hurt you, can you speak gently and encourage me and not just give me data rapid fire? When you take that tone it makes me feel like you want to shame me." I was a bit confused, but I responded, "Okay." What I learned was that when I get hurt, even though I measure my words carefully, I do not guard my tone well. It can sound intense and come off as harsh. I did not want her to feel belittled, so I had to learn to speak with more gentleness. We both learned from this incident to respect each other's feelings and adapted our actions as a result.

If you can learn to communicate well with each other, you will navigate through a lot of issues quickly. But if every disagreement dissolves into arguments and yelling, you need to pump the breaks. Before you jump into "till death do us part," make sure you pick up the skill of communication.

Survive a Moment of Confession

I believe there comes a moment before two people get engaged when they will need to look at each other and say, "Before we link our lives up forever, I need you to know some things about me. Not just the things you see. Not just the parts of me that I want to project to the world. But I need you to know about some of the broken things in me and some of the broken things in my past." Let me warn you: this will be a hard conversation. For some this will involve divulging sins that were committed against you. You may need to talk about past abuse you have suffered and how it might impact that way you approach conflict, money, or sex. For all of us it will involve confessing sins that we have committed. For some this will involve relationships that we were a part of in the past that were not healthy or decisions we made with our bodies or money that were not best. You must be able to share these things with each other. This does not need to be a running conversation over months. That can be needlessly painful.

Yet, I do believe strongly that there must come a time, a single conversation—or perhaps one large conversation with a few follow-ups—where you can divulge the secrets of your past.

Some of you may balk at this. *Isn't that my business? Why would I want to share that with my future spouse?* Because what they say in Alcoholics Anonymous is true: "We are only as sick as our secrets."[1] Concealing our transgressions from the one closest to us isn't a healthy way to start a marriage. You don't want to have to constantly redact comments to your spouse to make sure you don't accidentally divulge information about your previous life. That would be an exhausting way to live! You want to be able to have the freedom in your home to know that all the doors of your life are open.

Now, let me be quick to say, you do not want to have this deep conversation about your brokenness on a first date. I strongly discourage that. You don't even need to have it on date number ten. But somewhere down the road, if you think you all are journeying to the two-become-one stage of commitment, you need to have a moment where you don't give them every sordid detail but you do tell them about what has happened to you and about the things you've done. You reveal to them all those secret things in your heart you have been scared about a spouse finding out.

Why do this? Let me give you a couple direct benefits. First, it signals to the other person that you trust them, even with the most broken parts of you. That's scary. To let someone in to the most insecure places means you trust them. Second, it holds the potential to be powerfully healing. Proverbs 28:13 says, "Whoever conceals his transgressions will not prosper, but he who confesses and forsakes them will obtain mercy." Healing is possible when you can share with the one you love the most broken parts of you, and they are given the opportunity to respond with any of the following:

"I am sorry that happened."

"I forgive you."

"I love you."

"I still want you."

When you share the most wounded and broken parts of you and they respond with empathy and mercy, it can be a powerfully healing moment. Confessing and repenting opens the doors for restoration. It has the potential to take much of the sting out of old wounds in your life. Last, honest conversation about wounds from your past can greatly increase bonding. Not only does confession and mercy knit together some of the broken spaces inside of you, it can knit the two of you together in a stronger union. When you come to realize that this person already knows the worst about you and still loves you, it will greatly increase your confidence that the relationship has what it takes to survive any storm. Trust deepens. Confession also allows the other person the opportunity to love you with a Christlike love. Jesus Christ loved us at our worst and sacrificed himself for us when we were our worst. And he continues to patiently forgive us when we are at our worst. Christian marriage is meant to reflect this kind of Christlike love. Scripture teaches us, "[Forgive] one another, as God in Christ forgave you" (Ephesians 4:32). Experiencing this with the one you love will fasten you together deeply. If you discover this person can't forgive you, then praise God you figured that out on this side of marriage. You want a husband who is like Jesus, who grabbed us at our dirtiest and loved us. You want a wife like Jesus, who will see you in all your brokenness and extend grace and love toward you anyway. You need that.

Before we leave this subject, let me strongly encourage you: do not initiate a conversation about delicate subjects like abuse or sexual brokenness without first consulting wise counsel. Let some mature voices speak into your life, helping you discern how to best have this conversation. What would be the best way to bring it up? What level of detail about past experiences qualifies as sufficient to be a legitimate confession without going into unnecessarily graphic or hurtful detail? In programs like Alcoholics Anonymous, those working the process of recovery will begin by giving a First Step Presentation. This is a moment when they share with a trustworthy crowd their history with addiction, the nature of their past acting-out behaviors, and the damage they've done. Before this is shared, however, the addict works on the presentation along with a trusted sponsor who helps them craft the language to be honest about their past without heaping abuse upon themselves. The goal is to share enough for it to be a legitimate confession, but to leave out unnecessarily graphic detail. You will want to do the same. Before you and your potential spouse have a conversation of this significance, let someone who is wise help you think through how to talk about your past in a constructive way.

This brings us to our last point.

Support of Your Community

Proverbs 11:14 says, "Where there is no guidance, a people falls, but in an abundance of counselors there is safety." You do not need everybody around you giving you advice when you get married. My wife and I were both on staff at churches, and I remember I tried to keep secret that we were dating for as long as possible. This was not because I was embarrassed of her, nor because I wanted her to be my secret friend, but because I was at a church in the suburbs and I was the single guy at the church. So news of this nature always had a way of traveling too fast.

I saw our relationship like a fragile little flower peeking up from the dirt. I knew a lot of well-meaning people who, if they found out I was dating, would try to expedite the process. They would be tempted to grab that little flower and tug it upward, while shouting, "Grow young love! Grow!" I did not need that kind of drama.

But I did need counselors. I sought out a few healthy married couples and some good friends who I knew loved me enough to be straight with me. I told them I wanted them around and I wanted them to know everything to evaluate along with me. If they saw problem areas or a lack of health, they could call them out. I would strongly recommend you do the same. What is it that will give you increased confidence you are ready to transition from dating to engagement? The voices of the wise around you who can agree with you that this relationship is a good thing. When the chorus of the wise sound their approval, you can cross that threshold into marriage with confidence.

* * *

As I sat in that seminary library in Dallas, I went through my mental checklist. Not only did all of my good friends approve of Donna, but they adored her. They also watched us interact and believed we were a good complement to each other. She and I had processed through our pasts together, and we both expressed a deep resolve to commit even after knowing all the good and the bad. And when I looked within, I realized I wanted to be with her and only her. The benefits of being with Donna far outweighed the losses of freedom that come with singleness. Immediately after I wrapped up finals I drove through the night to speak to her father and tell him my intentions. As I sped along the freeway toward her dad's home, I was so filled with joy that I began to sing aloud from a heart filled with confidence because I knew that I knew I had the right one. I want that for you too!

The step from singleness to engagement is massive. Many

people today delay engagement because of the fear that they could be missing something or messing something up. Engagement is a leap of faith—trusting that you have found the right person to love you until death do you part. And yet it need not be a blind leap. But if you have these waypoints to navigate by—commitment, communication, confession, and community—you enter this exciting relational phase with confidence.

9

becoming one

"Babe, I'll be back in a few hours. I need to help your dad with a dead body."

Donna was sitting in the living room with her stepmom. We had driven together up to her dad's home in Oklahoma to bring the news to them that we had gotten engaged. We brought gifts to celebrate our impending union and invite them to be a part of the wedding. But before that moment, I was invited to be a part of something entirely unexpected: dressing a corpse.

Turns out Donna's dad was a mortician. A young man had passed away in a tragic accident, and her father had to hurry to the office to dress the body for a viewing. With little notice he did not have time to enlist his usual help. His most reliable employee had also asked to avoid the job, since he knew the deceased. So before I knew it, a few hours into the celebration of our impending nuptials, I was in a hearse on my way to the morgue. I remember thinking as we drove along, *Wow, I did not sign up for this.* But then I corrected myself. *Yes, I did.*

When you decide you want to marry someone, your lives merge.

All of your lives.

Engagement is a union. Your finances, your futures, and your families become one. And though your engagement might not begin with a ride in a hearse like mine, make no mistake, every wedding is also a funeral. Your single life is passing away, and a new, united life is emerging. The fun parts and the not-as-much-fun parts. Therefore, we need to talk about navigating this focused season of engagement when the two disappear and your lives begin the process of becoming one.

> **Your single life is passing away, and a new, united life is emerging.**

If you are reading this and are engaged, congratulations! Welcome to the best and worst part of your life. The best because you have identified The One. You have located the person with whom you want to spend the rest of your life. And that person wants to spend the rest of his or her life with you too.

Now, let me also welcome you to the worst part of your life. You will now enter a season where you will take on a majority share of the responsibilities of marriage, and only a few of its privileges. Get ready for months of event planning, budgeting, and navigating potentially complex family dynamics. But no living together. And no sex! What a wonderful combo. Prepare to suffer, my sweet friend.

Yet, here is the good news: friends will gather to encourage you. Loved ones will speak words of blessing over your life. And you will have a few months where the world expects you and your beloved to take time together to engage actively in the work of *union*. We call it being engaged, which is a great verb. It leads to a natural question: What am I engaged in? Let me answer that for you. You are engaged in a merger. Two formerly independent entities are fusing together. Linking families. Linking finances. And linking futures. This can be a delightful process of knowing each other deeply and being more deeply known, or it can be a rough one.

Think of it like the docking of a ship. You have been sailing the seas of singleness, and now you have finally found your port of call. You are coming home. A skilled captain will slowly let off the throttle so that the ship comes gently into port and fits like a glove alongside the dock. A less-skilled sailor can crash the ship into the dock and send wood and goods flying into the ocean. It all depends on how assured you are behind the wheel. It's the same with engagement. It can go smoothly or it can go poorly based entirely on your development of the skills of merging.

Engagement is about *union*—bringing the two together in every respect (except sex . . . not yet!). How can you merge in a way that you can step easily from singleness into marriage? How can you avoid unnecessary friction and conflict? Engagement focuses primarily on the union of three key areas of your lives:

Family
Finances
Future

Family

When you have figured out you love someone and want to spend the rest of your life with that person, you need to talk to his or her family. Some of you protest, "That's so old-fashioned! Who needs them?" Let me assure you I am in no way trying to uphold tradition. I am trying to invest in you wisdom. Proverbs 10 says, "A wise son makes a glad father, but a foolish son is a sorrow to his mother" (v. 1). This counts for son-in-laws as well! You want to bring your new family gladness, not sorrow. How do you do that? If you are going to join your life together with someone else, you will also be joining your families together. Their parents will be related to you until you die. If you have children, you will be the parent of their grandchildren, and they will be the grandparents of your kids. That's where you are headed. Therefore it is wise to get off on the right foot. You want to start with a good relational foundation because you will most likely see these people every Christmas for the rest of their lives.

It is wise to let them see that you two have a healthy relationship. If their fears are allayed, you have given them the opportunity to be supportive of your marriage rather than suspicious of it. People value access. They will value being invited in. VIP sections. Special seating. Parties. Events. People like being invited to things, even if they decline the invitation. It honors them when they know they have been thought of and included. In the same way, by inviting each other's parents to come and see your new relationship, you honor them. This is a wise move. It is also easier for them to celebrate your relationship if they have a chance to evaluate it up close.

I remember several years ago a young man I had mentored for a few years sent me an e-mail. In it he quickly explained that he had met the love of his life while in Europe and he would love for me to officiate their wedding. Was I willing? I did not want to pour water on the fire of his enthusiasm, but I did have to send him an e-mail that was a bit cautious. I do not officiate many weddings. And I like to know the couple and feel confident that their relationship is solid before I stand up publicly and endorse it. So rather than send him a hearty congratulations, I sent him a list of questions so I could (1) evaluate whether or not they were a good fit and (2) feel a peace of mind as I celebrate their union. It is hard to celebrate what you have not had the opportunity to evaluate. After reading the treatise he wrote back, and meeting her a few months later, I found it easy to celebrate their union along with them.

A gift you can give your soon-to-be in-laws is to let them in. Let them see your chemistry—that you make their child happy. And let them see you have character—that you are a responsible human being who will care and provide for their child. They need to see both if you want them to celebrate.

This is where I have seen many younger men go wrong. Throughout my twelve years living and working among college students, I visited with several young men who arrived in my office seeking advice on damage control. They met with a young woman's parents and it did not go well. When I ask about what happened, they usually recount the story of how they fell in love with this girl and decided that they needed to be married ASAP. So he drove to her parents' home and declared to her father, "I love your daughter!" To which he replied, "A lot of people love my daughter." "Oh, well, of course. But I want to marry her." "I don't know you, son. Do you even have a job?" And an awkward, tense conversation ensued. I've talked to guys who are confused as to why it went down like that. Or I have had some guys come to me asking for biblical support for defying her parents' wishes and getting married anyway while they are young. When I press, they usually confide that her dad has demanded that his daughter get a degree before she get married. So they are looking for a way to quote the Bible at her father to defy his request and get the girl.

Here is my typical response to that anxious young man: "You need to understand something. Not too long ago in his mind, that man and his wife had a baby. In that moment when his eyes first met his daughter, a part of his heart sprang to life. He discovered a deep, profound love in himself for his little baby girl. Then, seconds later, he remembered what a harsh, dangerous, twisted world we live in. In that moment he swore to himself and to the universe that he would protect and provide for this little girl with everything he has. Now you have come along and essentially said to him, "Hey, give me that baby!" But you have, to this point, done absolutely nothing to convince this man that you are anything but a threat. He is supposed to be protective. Thus, he is supposed to be wary of you. That's his job.

When my oldest daughter was four years old, I was helping her one morning put on her shoes before she headed off to pre-school. As I tied the laces, she said, "Tony is going to love these." Immediately I responded, "Who is Tony?" I looked at my wife, "WHO IS TONY?" She said, "Relax. He is a boy from school." But there was no relaxing. Instantly the thoughts sprang to my mind, *I don't know him. And frankly, I don't care what Tony thinks about your shoes. And I don't think you need to care about what Tony thinks about anything! You know what, I don't know who this Tony character is, but if he's got some ideas about you in his mind I want to know. What are his intentions? Who does he think he is? He'd better not have another single thought about your shoes until he talks to me. You tell Tony I'm not afraid to go back to jail. You hear me! It's not a problem for me!* But I kept all that inside. I just said something to her like, "Tell me all about Tony, baby." Why? Because he is a threat to me. If he wants influence in my daughter's life, I want to know him and approve of his influence. You will save everyone a lot of stress if you can prioritize meeting each other's parents. Let them get to know you. And show them that you would like to know them. Union with family is not simply about letting them see you, but it's about you seeing them.

Ephesians 6 says, "Honor your father and mother" (v. 2). This includes father-in-laws and mother-in-laws. How do you honor someone? I'll tell you an easy way: value what that person values. How can you show them you care about what they care about? With your words and with your wealth, that's how. To do so with your words, when you meet the parents, show them that you value their role as influencer in their child's life. How? By asking them questions. People like to talk about themselves. If you are genuinely interested in them as human beings, that will establish trust. I am *not* telling you to be manipulative. I am telling you how to be polite. When you meet them, a way you can show them you care is by being genuinely interested in them as human beings. Don't just roll in with your agenda. Ask questions and listen. Then celebrate anything and everything in their life that you can celebrate. Certainly, don't celebrate sin in their lives—if they have a drinking problem or if they are overly cynical. But look for the things you can celebrate and then do it. Does he like movies? Ask about which ones he loves and why. Does she love decorating? Then ask her about it! I remember when Donna was living with an older family who were like parents to her; the mom loved decorating the kitchen with frogs. Hundreds of frogs. So I asked about them. Do I have a great passion for frog-based decor? No. But she clearly did, so I asked! Turns out the frogs help her think about relying on God (I think it was the acronym Fully Rely On God). They had a tragedy in their family, and surrounding herself with reminders of God's faithfulness helped her cope. By asking a question about something surface, we were able to get to something deeper. And as I genuinely cared about her interests, her family, her heart, and her pain, she learned that she could trust me. You can do the same. Whether the conversation stays surface or goes deep, value what they value. Take interest in what they are interested in. It builds trust. Then, in the immortal words of Jerry Maguire, "Show them the money."

Finances

When you look at the book of Proverbs, it's a father pleading with his son, encouraging him to be wise. One of the areas stressed most often is wealth. How do you handle money? Let me tell you something, young men: when you arrive to that family, those parents have cared for that girl and provided for that girl for decades. When you ask for her hand in marriage, you are essentially saying to her parents, "Hand over your baby girl and pay forty thousand dollars to do it [the current average cost of a wedding in the United States]." How are you going to win that one?

Show them that you are not a predator but a protector right along with them. Let them know you will care for and protect for their child emotionally. Then, show them the money. Let them know that you have thought through how to pay the bills. I talk to many young couples who come to me and say, "We want to get married." I always ask next, "Can you afford it?" Often, younger couples will say something along the lines of, "Oh, we will figure that out. We're going to live on love!" Unfortunately, love doesn't pay the bills, kids. But love should propel you to figure out how to pay the bills.

I often encourage young couples to sit down with an accountant or with a parent or some other trusted older person in their community who is good with money. And I challenge them to come up with a budget. Figure out what it costs for two people to live. This is a profound reality check for young couples. They aren't sure how much an apartment will cost. They are unaware that insurance will cost more for a married couple. Often when I challenge young men to come up with a budget, they realize they are not in a position to care for a woman. At that point I tell them, "Well, now you have a goal."

I have sat with others who took a finance class or did a Dave

Ramsey seminar. They worked up a budget and figured out that they do in fact have enough to live on together. This is good for you because it shows that you know how to manage your household well. It will also increase your confidence as you sit down with each other's families. Then you can come into that meeting with each other's parents and say, "We love each other. We want to care for and support each other in every conceivable way. With regards to finances, we have worked up a budget and have saved enough that we believe we can adequately care for each other." Then, particularly if you are young, you may want to even show them the budget. If you are older and have a steady job, that may not be necessary. But you still, in that event, want to find a way to tell them that you have worked up a budget that is sustainable. It communicates honor to them. Their number one goal is that their baby is provided for. You have shown them that you value that goal, enough to have thought through it ahead of time in detail and arrived at this moment prepared. I can't stress this enough, particularly to young men. You want the blessing of her parents. Show them not only that you want to care for their daughter but that *you can*. This is a great gift to give each other's families. It will greatly reduce their stress and greatly increase the likelihood that they will celebrate your union rather than urge caution.

This exercise of working on finances is not just good for the future in-laws, it is strengthening for the marriage as well. The greatest cause of stress in a marriage is finances.[1] Not just the question of whether or not there is enough money, but how we want to spend it. You will likely come in with different thoughts about giving, saving, and spending. Maybe you have not thought much about any of it. Maybe one of you has a very detailed budget and one does not. Maybe you have very different priorities. One of you has a small clothing budget, but a sizable amount of resources allocated toward the latest technology. Maybe the other loves buying clothes, but doesn't care much about the latest TV. Maybe one is a big saver and the other a big spender. These can be sources of great stress if you stumble into them repeatedly throughout the first years of marriage. Better to prepare ahead of time. You know the bills are coming. You know money will flow into and out of your lives. Wisdom dictates that you begin at this point to figure out how you will allocate funds as a couple.

There are great resources out there for young couples to work through their budgets. I encourage you to tap into those resources and work up a budget together. Take a premarital class, buy a premarital counseling book, and work on your family budget together. It will unearth your priorities and give you an opportunity to figure out what your family cares about and how that will be reflected in where your money goes. Money can be a cause of great stress or great celebration in a young couple. Whether there is joy or anxiety is often based not on how much money comes in or out, but on how well that money is managed. Work now on stewarding your resources well, and I promise, you will greatly reduce stress and greatly increase satisfaction in your early years of marriage.

Future

As you prepare for marriage, you are uniting your families, your finances, and your futures. You are running into the unknown together. During those months of engagement, take time each week to look up from the immediate wedding plans and work on your plans for your marriage. Donna and I tried to find one night a week where we did not talk about the wedding at all. We just talked about the marriage. I tried to come to those evenings with some conversation starters. Some of the questions I brought to the table were:

How do we want to do the holidays?

Will we see all our in-laws each holiday, or work a
rotation system?

What holiday traditions do we want to bring into our
marriage?

What new traditions do we want to create?

How do we want to do vacations?

Where are some places you have always wanted to go?

How many kids do you want to have? How soon?

How are we going to budget our time each week?

Will we have a date night?

How will we plan our budget and make financial
decisions? When? How frequently?

What are some ministry dreams you have?

How can we make those happen?

How will we cultivate a devotional life together?

How will we handle car maintenance?

What about house cleaning and yard work?

Use this time of engagement to ask questions like these so you can minimize friction in the first years of marriage.

For Donna and me, our time of engagement, particularly of getting to know each other's families, actually served to do wonders within our respective families. Some people in both of our families were cynical about marriage as an institution. They had only seen it done poorly. But as they saw us interact with each other with not only infatuation, but wisdom, their hope seemed to rise. Others who were cynical about religion saw how our faith provided a steady foundation for our relationship and it challenged them to reexamine their beliefs.

For others of you, interacting with each other's families may sharpen you as well. I remember the first wedding I cried at. It was a direct result of a moment that occurred during the rehearsal dinner the night before. After several minutes of family and friends offering encouragement and blessings to the bride and groom, the husband-to-be stood up at the end of the evening and thanked everyone for coming. He then recounted to everyone the story of how rocky their engagement had been. He had designed to marry this young girl, but they had done very little thinking through any of the issues we have discussed above. He told the story of

> ## Ask questions so you can minimize friction in the first years of marriage.

her parents' extreme hesitation about blessing their marriage. Then the young groom said to his soon-to-be father-in-law, "I remember all those nights I sat for hours on your couch, talking about how to be a husband who cares for his wife. I hated that couch. But as I look back now, it was an anvil and God shaped me on it and made me into the man I am. Thank you."

Faith

What a relief to be nearing the shore when you have been on a long voyage. Yet every sailor knows that often a vessel is in greatest danger as it comes into port. Rocks, shoals, and reefs lurk just beneath the surface of the water that can do incredible damage to a ship. The same is true of relationships. What a euphoric relief to have found the one—and to have that person love you back!

And yet the wise couple sees that these final months before marriage require great wisdom in navigating the hidden troubles that can come from uniting families, finances, and future plans. This takes great skill.

Or it takes simple faith.

In 1989, the massive oil tanker *Exxon Valdez* crashed into a reef off the shore of Prince William Sound in Alaska, spilling more than ten million gallons of oil into the ocean. The spill, covering more than 11,000 square miles of ocean and 1,300 miles of coastline, caused massive damage to the local wildlife. Analysis of what went wrong revealed that faulty equipment and inadequately prepared sailors led to the catastrophe. So how did the country respond? Do all tankers coming into port come equipped with state-of-the-art equipment and the best sailors? I don't know. But it also may not matter that much. After the spill, laws were passed that require all tankers coming in and out of Prince William Sound to be towed in by a tugboat helmed by a captain who possesses intimate knowledge of the challenges of the port. For tankers in Alaska now, success has come through surrender. They find their way home safely by tethering themselves to the one who has the expertise and ability to guide them safely to port. You can do the same.

This brief moment of engagement can be tough. A million decisions must be made about everything from what city you will live in to the choice of font on your thank-you notes—all while you are in many ways still getting to know each other! There is plenty of danger you can crash into. Yet you don't have to be brilliant to be wise. You need only tether yourself to the One who knows how to navigate the complexities of life and love. Trust that the Lord who designed marriage knows how to best enter into it. Consider praying every day for your impending union. And read back over the verses from throughout this section and do what they say! To be tethered to God in faith means that I also believe that the way he says to do things really is the best way. I promise as you listen to and live out his counsel, you will find great success in uniting your families, finances, and futures.

10

an engagement case study

solomon + the shulammite // song of solomon

One of the most beautiful books in the Bible is the Song of Solomon. It consists of a collection of songs written by or about King Solomon, concerning his courtship, wedding, and marriage with his beloved Shulammite. Rather than warning against all the dangers of misplaced love or lust, the Song of Solomon portrays a couple who does it right. They are passionate and pure. Holy and hot. So hot in fact that young Jewish boys were not allowed to read this book until they were of a certain age. It extols the beauties of love in all of its passion, and it can make you blush with its unashamed celebration of sex.

Early in the book we get a song recounting the days when these young lovers began to grow in their affection for one another and move toward marriage. Though it is beyond the scope of this chapter to journey throughout the entire book, we can glean some insights as we consider what we should see and feel in a relationship that gives us the confidence we are with the right person.

Excitement

How do you know you are ready to marry someone? An initial indicator is *excitement!* In the beginning of Song of Solomon the two lovers' excitement leaps from the page. The book begins with her provocative exclamation, "Let him kiss me with the kisses of his mouth!" (1:2). When we meet this girl, we already know she desires this man. She essentially shouts to the world, "I want his mouth on my mouth!" Is it wrong to desire someone? NO! God designed attraction and this woman is unashamedly infatuated. She declares that his love is better than wine (v. 2). Wine was the drink of celebration. In the ancient world it was one of the most enjoyable things they could taste. It could make your insides feel warm and your head feel light. The way this man treats her elicits a similar response. Now a natural question to ask at this point would be: *What has this man done to get this girl so dialed up?*

She declares in the next verse, "Your anointing oils are fragrant" (v. 3). She could just be saying that his cologne game is working for her. The Middle East is hot. People get sweaty. And back then they did not have frequent showers. So men would wear aromatic oils. But as the verse continues, you realize there is more going on here than his scent. She explains, "Your name is oil poured out" (v. 3). What does that mean?

The poetry of the statement is brilliant. Scent is our sense most tied to memory. It also provokes a response. If you love the scent of something, you move closer. You breathe out, "Mmm." You respond. Likewise, if something stinks, you pull away. You might even wrinkle up your nose as an attempt to retreat from the odor. You don't map out these responses. They are just instinctive and undeniable.

The names of people are the same way. When someone's name is spoken, you have an instinctual response. What are you responding to? What instantly comes to mind for you is not even so much the memory of that person, but a feeling you get as you consider that person's attributes. When I say, "Hitler," you are very likely to recoil. Do you think about any of his speeches? No. You are just reacting to a general impression you have based on his character.

When the Shulammite hears this man's name, she thinks of his reputation; she sees his character. Images flash into her mind of his

Marry character. Let that be what turns you on.

kindness. His presence is pleasant. Ladies, what should draw you to a man? His character. His looks will fade. His hairline will recede. His nose and earlobes will continue to grow. His rear will oddly shrivel up. Don't base your romantic relationships on looks. That is the area that will the most assuredly fade. Is the guy you are attracted to impatient? Is he a bad listener? Is he selfish with his money? Do you think he will suddenly become a scent of sweetness when you get older? That is unlikely.

Proverbs 22:1 says, "A good name is more desirable than great riches; to be esteemed is better than silver or gold" (NIV). Marry character. Let that be what turns you on.

Are you unsure of how to identify character? Then get some quality voices around you. In the Song of Solomon, four voices speak: God, the man, the woman, and the woman's friends. Why? Because that is how it always is, boys. If you want to win the girl, you've got to win the stamp of approval from her squad. The first time I asked my future wife, Donna, on a date, she asked me to pick her up at her church. When I arrived, I was greeted by no less than one hundred people. She worked with the youth and they had been leading an event for high school students. Over the next hour I met every man and woman, young and old, that worked on staff or as a volunteer at that church. I discovered later this was by design. Before she ever got in a car with me, even though we had talked several times before, she wanted her community to have an opportunity to evaluate me. Wise woman. The Shulammite from Song of Solomon does the same. She wants her friends to evaluate this man.

They concur with her assessment of him in the following verse: "We will exult and rejoice in you; we will extol your love more than wine; rightly do they love you" (1:4). What they are essentially saying to their friend is, "He is a worthy person upon which to set your affections. Your affections are rightly placed." Godly love has excitement, but it is excitement stirred by character.

Thank God Donna did not just marry me because she thought I was attractive. A few years into our marriage I injured my back. During recovery from surgery I gained more than thirty pounds, and not a single pound of it was muscle! Later, when I reinjured my back, I lost fifty pounds and became sickly thin. If she was only into looks, I would have been in trouble. We are happily married because she was drawn to character, and because she possesses character as well. Don't settle for less. But character alone is not enough. The couple in Song of Solomon is also stirred by one another's kindness.

In chapter 2 we see the man's excitement. The Shulammite

declares, "Behold, he comes, leaping over the mountains, bound-ing over the hills. My beloved is like a gazelle or a young stag. Behold, there he stands behind our wall, gazing through the windows, looking through the lattice" (2: 8–9). Notice: he is not walking to her house. He is bounding like a gazelle and radiating masculinity like a young stag. No mountain can obstruct him. Nothing will deter him from reaching his beloved! And when he arrives he searches anxiously to get a glimpse of her. Why is he so fired up?

In verse 10 he speaks, saying to her, "Arise, my love, my beau-tiful one." The Hebrew word we translate "love" from here is the word *rayahti*. Used throughout the Old Testament, the word is variously translated, "neighbor", "companion," or "friend." Yes, he is attracted to her physically, referring to her as a beautiful one. But nine times throughout this short book he chooses to call her "friend." She refers to him throughout the text as *dodi*, translated here as "beloved." It carries a similar idea of someone cherished. What this means is that they are drawn to one another's char-acter, but they are also knit closer and closer together by their continued kindness and friendship. They simply enjoy being with one another.

I have sat through several meals with couples where both the man and woman were physically attractive, and at least one of them wealthy. But within minutes it became painfully apparent they did not seem to connect at a relational level very well. They talked over one another, misunderstood each other, or annoyed and simply tolerated one another. I have even sat with couples who outwardly criticize each other. I can't imagine continuing down the road toward marriage with someone I did not feel a sense of kinship and goodwill. Putting on a ring will not suddenly make a person kind, sensitive, or interesting. But the years *will* take his or her looks. How do you know you're meant to be with someone? There is an ease to it, you want to be together, and communication does not feel like an obligation. The other person is your friend. But it is not only about enjoying your beloved's company, it is also about being improved by his or her company.

Life

Notice Solomon's language as he calls this woman to come away with him.

> My beloved speaks and says to me:
> "Arise, my love, my beautiful one,
> and come away,
> for behold, the winter is past;
> the rain is over and gone.
> The flowers appear on the earth,
> the time of singing has come,
> and the voice of the turtledove
> is heard in our land.
> The fig tree ripens its figs,
> and the vines are in blossom;
> they give forth fragrance.
> Arise, my love, my beautiful one,
> and come away. (vv. 10–13)

I remember when I first heard Tommy Nelson preach this text. He asked a room full of women, "What time of year is this?" Without hesitation, a chorus of voices responded, "Spring!" I believe Tommy's assessment of this moment is correct: Solomon poetically ties their budding romance to the first days of spring because, like their surroundings, their relationship is brimming with life.

How do you know your relationship is headed toward marriage? Not only is there a growing emotional excitement, but your time together promotes growth in one another's lives. For me this becomes an obvious indicator when I watch couples date. With some couples you see their continued communication bring out the best in one another. The other person challenges them to engage God in new ways. Both parties want to be the best version of themselves whenever they are around the other. They are both challenged to grow spiritually. They spur one another on toward love and good deeds.

On the other end of the spectrum, I have seen others begin to date and over time their joy fades. They seem burdened. Weighed down. A sense of guilt covers them. They begin to distance from community. They withdraw. Their attitudes become more cynical. In some cases it might be because one of them drags the other down. At other times, I have seen both individuals walk with the Lord and other people but they just weren't ready for a romantic relationship. Lack of healthy boundaries physically saddles them with guilt and robs them of vibrancy. Poor communication fills their life with stress. This was me in college. I dated some great girls, but I just wasn't ready for a relationship. I had too many issues in my own life that needed tending to. Like my friend Gregg Matte has said, "The right person at the wrong time is the wrong person." Sometimes you just need to be honest enough with yourself to say that you are not ready to be in a serious relationship.

This seems like an obvious point but it deserves to be stated directly: you may be great individuals, but if the net result of your union is negative in your lives and in the lives of others you don't want to bind yourselves together in marriage. Why put yourself in a hurt locker for the rest of your life? How much more fun will the future be if the person closest to you is constantly challenging you to be the best man, woman, friend, child, parent, minister, or child of God you can possibly be? You want your relationship to be synergistic. The combination of your lives produces life by uplifting the spirits of those around you.

Trust

This couple has arrived at that moment where they are increasingly convinced this is the person they want to marry. Attraction has been replaced by love, and like every plant in its early stages, their relationship has entered a vulnerable moment. It is growing but there is a fragility present too. When you go on a few dates with someone the most you risk is a little time and some money. But when you begin to intentionally evaluate one another, now there is the potential to be hurt. But for a relationship to grow a young couple must risk the vulnerability without which there will be no depth.

The couple in Song of Solomon is willing to take the risk, so the man calls for the woman to come away with him. Listen to the invitation:

O my dove, in the clefts of the rock, in the crannies of the cliff, let me see your face, let me hear your voice, for your voice is sweet, and your face is lovely. (v. 14)

Notice the imagery. She is described as something beautiful and tender—a dove. She is also pictured as high up in the cleft of a rock. She is out of reach. Inaccessible. But he does not scale the cliff to try to snatch the dove. He speaks tenderly. Gently, he calls for her to come forth. This is the perfect depiction of the delicate dance of young love. He desires intimacy with her. He wants to know her more. But this is a request for her to be vulnerable, so it is risky. What if she shares her innermost thoughts, hopes, dreams, and desires and he takes off? That hurts tremendously. And many of you know that hurt. There should be a reticence when someone wants to have access to the deepest parts of you. Yet notice how he does it, gentlemen. He initiates. He invites. He compliments. He gets vulnerable first; sharing with her his heart honestly that he desires her. Then he waits for her to respond.

In my opinion, if you are not in a position where you feel you could get married in the next six months, then do not attempt to forge this level of intimacy. Gentlemen, don't come running up like a stag, peering through the lattice, and calling her to come away with you if you do not possess the maturity and stability to care for her. If this is the case, you are just a boy playing games. But you are playing them with the delicate soul of a woman. That is wrong and that is not loving. Do not call a young woman out from the cleft of the rock if your plan is to just "kinda see what happens" and maybe get a chance to grope her. Ladies, don't share the depths of your soul with a boy who isn't interested in or prepared for marriage. You are leaping into some hands that lack the maturity to handle you well. The apostle Peter called women the "weaker vessel" (1 Peter 3:7), which can sound insulting if misunderstood. The word *weaker* would be better translated *delicate*. It is not an insult. I would never use my iPad to dig a trench. Why? Because it is more sensitive equipment. That does not make it less valuable. In fact, it makes it more! In the same way, Solomon poetically captures what Peter bluntly states: there is a delicacy to the hearts of women. Men, be gentle. Ladies, be discerning.

Ladies, as you share more of your heart and he continues to treat you with kindness, and men, as you continue to initiate and she responds with encouragement and respect, you can both continue to move forward. I remember when this transition happened for Donna and me. The excitement of attraction blasted us off into the stratosphere, but when those boosters were expended the questions became, *Can we maintain an orbit together, or will we come crashing to earth? The more I get to know you, can I trust you with the depths of my heart? Are you a safe place for me?*

It is in these days of court-ship, and on into engagement, that you will share the heart-breaks of your past. You will tell each other honestly about what you used to be or what you have experienced. This is important. You do not want to surprise them later. Some of you will share pasts of abuse. Some of you will share deep regrets. These are typically

Spur each other on toward love and good deeds.

the moments when tears are shed. Some of you will discover that your beloved has been wounded deeply in the past, and you will want to pull them close. You can't rush this process any more than you can rush the growing of a flower. You can create conditions for it to flourish, but you must allow time. When you have the stability of two mature souls engaging in the vulnerability of sharing their hearts, you have created the conditions necessary for the growth of love and respect. Now all that remains is to see if this budding relationship is meant to flourish into a full-blown marriage.

As this couple in Song of Solomon grows closer emotionally, the natural inclination is to get together physically. But notice their response:

> Catch the foxes for us, the little foxes that spoil the vineyards,
> for our vineyards are in blossom. (2:15)

What does this mean? Well, foxes were hated in the ancient world. They would eat the buds of plants so that they could not bloom. In this passage, where their young love has been pictured as a garden, the foxes represent that which would be a threat to the relationship. The young couple calls for community support. They have a mutual commitment to remove threats to their relationship and they call on their community for assistance. Specifically, before their wedding night arrives you see a continual call for sexual restraint.

There is something very natural about wanting to progress from emotional bonding to physical bonding. Every young couple struggles with premarital sexual desire. If you aren't tempted, it's possible you have a whole different set of problems. But the reality remains, you do not know that someone is yours until you agree to the covenant of marriage. Until that covenant is made on your wedding day, his or her body is not yours. To the Corinthians Paul explained that the husband's body belongs to the wife and the wife's body belongs to the husband. Until you agree to take the responsibility of caring for a person emotionally, financially, spiritually, and physically, you should not get the benefits of enjoying his or her body sexually.

When I first entered college, I moved in with two guys whose girlfriends frequently stayed with us. I remember one of them stopping and asking me, "Do you think it's wrong that I'm sleeping with my girlfriend?" I was taken aback by his question. I responded, "I think my initial thought is that I am much more concerned about what kind of relationship you have with God. I think your relationship with your girlfriend would not be the first conversation I'd want to have." He responded, "Well, I think it's okay because we are going to get married anyway." They broke up later that semester. Actually, both couples broke up. Though it was a surprise to everyone, it was not beyond the realm of possibility. As serious as a dating relationship can feel, it can still dissolve in an afternoon. You are meant to pursue and enjoy sex, but within the context of a covenantal relationship.

In the next verse of the Song of Solomon, the Shulammite declares, "My beloved is mine, and I am his" (v. 16). She is expressing affection, but notice that it is with the language of ownership. *We belong to each other.* This is how sexuality is meant to be expressed—within the safety of promise. That is what a marriage is—the most serious promise we can make. It is to look someone in the eye and say, "I am committing all of me to you. And I want all of you." A boyfriend-girlfriend relationship, as close as it may feel, can only declare, "I might want all of you." Please don't give all of yourself away to someone whose best is a solid *maybe.* You want to give all of your passion to the person who says before God and the whole world, "I am holding nothing back from this other person. Relationally, financially, spiritually, and physically, I am yours." Marriage should be the place of full safety and full freedom. It is the place for the full donation of yourself sexually. That is the beauty of covenantal love. Anything less is too cheap.

This is why the young woman, as much as she desires this man, declares, "I adjure you, O daughters of Jerusalem, by the gazelles or the does of the field, that you not stir up or awaken love until it pleases" (2:7). Your passion is good. Just make sure it is well placed.

Too Wonderful to Explain

Donna and I met when I was twenty-six. I spoke at an event where her band led worship. It was a season of life during which I knew I was about to leave the youth ministry that I had shepherded for five years and head out to seminary somewhere in the continental U.S. I was in the midst of a major life transition, so the last thing I was looking to do was begin a relationship with someone in the town I knew I would not be living in.

But there she was.

In the few years prior to meeting Donna, I had prided myself in my ability to control romantic impulses and focus my time and energy on the work of ministry. I liked moving fast and working hard at eternal things. I did not want to chase girls.

But there she was.

I found myself trying to sit by her or accepting invitations to go out with her friend group so I could be around her. I found myself calling her cell phone and beginning to talk to her late at night. *What am I doing?* I realized after a few weeks that I was attracted to this woman. I could not fight it. I understood there would be commitments of time, energy, and resources to get to know her. I was willing to spend it. I understood there was risk of getting hurt emotionally. I found within myself a willingness to take the risk. I did not know how the timing would work. *What would we do when I move cities?* I decided that was a legitimate concern, but it was not a significant enough of an issue to warrant terminating the exploration of discerning whether we were built to be together. We began to see each other regularly. After a few nights of getting to know each other, it was clear the affection was there. But I had been attracted to people before. *How was I to know this was really the right one?*

We began to talk longer hours on the phone, getting to know one another. We spent more and more time together. I realized I did not just find her attractive or interesting. I sensed a kinship and a similar view of life. We were so different in key areas, but so similar in our passions to really live and to make our lives count. We began risking greater and greater revelations to one another about our pasts. We spent enough time together to run into disagreements. We experienced miscommunication and discovered within ourselves the desire to work through them to find resolution and reconnection. We didn't want barriers between us. Difficulties were not a signal that our lives were going different directions; they were an invitation to exert more energy to work toward connection. They were obstacles that were made to be overcome. They were tests that proved to ourselves and to one another that we truly wanted to be together.

I moved. That was a big test. Distance and time dissolve a lot of relationships. Paths diverge and the fragile relationship cannot handle the strain. We, however, found a desire within that would leap mountains to be with the other. And it was not just passion or lust. We were chaste. It was the deep desire of connection at a heart level. I found ways to make the late-night drives. To book the flights. To create the space. I found myself working on my calendar and on my finances to figure out how we could make this work.

When I felt that sense within me of *I don't just want sex, I want her*, and when I saw in her eyes that she wanted me, that made restraint sexually extremely difficult. We made sure we didn't spend long hours alone. I never went in her apartment. We had friends that would call us when they knew we would have longer hours alone in the car. There were moments, particularly after midnight, where it seemed to make all the sense in the world to express our growing desire for each other with physical touch. It felt wrong to deny the impulse.

But there were also mixed in a few moments where the challenges concerning how to reconcile our seemingly different directions and goals in key areas that threw the whole enterprise into question. *Was this right? Do our plans for the future align?* In those moments, when our paths seemed to diverge a little, it reminded me afresh that this woman was not mine. Not mine to hold. Not mine to take home. We had to continually submit our desires, plans, ambitions, and questions to the Lord.

So even though there were moments where we felt all but married, there were also enough moments sprinkled in along the way that convinced us afresh that there is no such thing as "essentially married." You either are or you are not. And we were not. So we continued to talk. To plan. To pray. We had to see what areas of our lives could bend toward the other. In time, we found out that we could make it work. My ministry path and hers were compatible and our personalities meshed well.

While we were dating, Donna and I realized that we had shared a meal together seven years earlier. I had traveled to Huntsville, Texas, with my mentor to help him evaluate a potential new worship leader for the ministry he led. After the service my mentor, Gregg, and I had dinner with the worship leader and his entire team. That worship leader happened to be Donna's boss. She was at that dinner. But, to our knowledge, Donna and I never spoke that night. We also discovered that I owned one of her band's albums. One of my friends had given it to me years ago and I had never opened it. I had even attended one of her concerts. But I walked in right as her set ended so I didn't hear her play. We discovered later that we brushed past each other that night, but hadn't seen each other's faces. All of these revelations on top of the fact that it turned out we already had literally dozens of mutual friends. But we had never met. A friend of mine told me once while I was single that she was praying for me to be like Adam. She prayed I would go about the work God had called me to do. Then, in God's perfect timing, he would open my eyes and I would see Eve. I believe God answered that prayer. I was not on a desperate search for Donna. But our individual pursuits of the Lord led us into proximity to one another at the right time.

And there she was.

I am praying he does the same for you. How will the particu-

larities of your story work out? It is impossible to say. The writer
Agur states in Proverbs 30:18–19:

> *Three things are too wonderful for me;*
> *four I do not understand:*
> *the way of an eagle in the sky,*
> *the way of a serpent on a rock,*
> *the way of a ship on the high seas,*
> *and the way of a man with a virgin.*

There is great mystery in the way a man and a woman come
to know one another. Our journeys into intimacy mirror a ship on
high seas far more than they do a car on a road. Each of our paths
will be unique. Yet, as you journey through your unique story of
initmacy, we can all navigate by the same stars. The same principles can guide us all. And when it comes to evaluating whether
or not you have found the right one in the right way, I adjure you:
look for excitement, life, and for a deepening of trust. And trust
God to guide you to the right one in the right way at the right
time. It makes for a beautiful story when you do.

married: mission

God designed marriage to be a picture of Jesus and a pursuit of Jesus. In this way, marriage reaches its fullest potential. The strongest bonds are formed when a man and a woman live out their marriage on mission together.

11

marriage as a picture

On September 19, 2014, Apple launched the iPhone 6. Three days later, more than thirteen million were already in use.[1] Not only had Apple succeeded in making an incredible product, it had masterfully marketed it. Millions watched breathlessly as the CEO announced the latest phone and its incredible new features. Yet, if you watch the presentation, you will notice that he did not say, "Note how this elegant piece of machinery can be jammed under a door as a door-stop. We are revolutionizing room-entry." Or, "Note how the sleek design allows it to smoothly spread butter across toast." Why? Because that was not what it was created for! The makers of the iPhone understand that the highest potential will be reached and the greatest satisfaction experienced if its creation is used in accordance with its design. This is true of all things. *Freedom is not the absence of boundaries, it is the ability to fulfill created intent.* A fish is most free when it swims. A bird is most free when it flies. For all of life, the highest potential will be achieved, and the greatest satisfaction experienced, if we live in accordance with our Creator's intended design.

The same is true of marriage. When we enter a marriage relationship, we are participating in an institution that God designed. Therefore, our greatest potential and our highest satisfaction in marriage will be achieved when we engage in it in a way consistent with his design. This leads to the important question: What is marriage for? We need to look to the One *who* made it and discern *why* he made it to understand *how* to do it well.

Marriage: Designed by God

We first see God's design for marriage in Genesis 2. As God fashioned all of creation, he declared seven times that "it is good." But, then, in verse 18 we get our first "not good." God said, "It is not good that the man should be alone." The animals were already there with Adam, but let's be honest, there is a big difference between watching a sunset with a beautiful woman and watching it with a cocker spaniel. More than that, God did not intend for man to simply be a cul-de-sac for God's love and grace. Man is meant to be a conduit of love and grace flowing into other relationships.

God fashioned from the side of Adam what Genesis calls "a helper suitable for him" (2:18 NASB). One that was a good fit. What 1 Peter calls "a fellow heir of the grace of life" (3:7 NASB). Different from each other, yet made to fit together. Physically (obviously), but also spiritually and emotionally. God designs husbands and wives to complement each other—to fit together in a way that brings joy to them both. God designed marriage for our delight. As God walked Eve to Adam, the man spontaneously broke out in rhyme. And the curtain closes on Genesis 2 with a man and woman completely vulnerable with each other and completely at peace.

This is the design of marriage. It is a good gift from God. When we engage marriage in accordance with God's design, there is safety and delight, and we flourish.

Some may ask, "Wait, don't Christians get divorced as often as non-Christians do? Why would I take the 'Christian' way of marrying seriously if it does not seem to work?" W. Bradford Wilcox, a leading sociologist at the University of Virginia and the director of National Marriage Project, created a separate category in his research for those he refers to as "Active Conservative Protestants." *Active* meaning that they are involved in a local church. *Conservative* does not mean politically, but theologically. In short, they believe the Bible is the Word of God. *Protestants* meaning that they believe we are saved from our sin by the grace of God available in Jesus Christ. His research indicates that Active Conservative Protestants are 35 percent less likely to divorce than their counterparts.[2]

> **God designs a husband and wife to complement each other.**

In short, those who depend upon the grace of God and take his Word seriously have considerably stronger marriages. It is wise to listen to the Creator's intent for marriage. People who walk through marriage in accordance with God's design find that his ways work.

Marriage Displays God

What is even more exciting is that God designed this institution with a great end goal in mind. Marriage is not just designed *by God*; it is meant to display something *about God*.

When Paul quoted the passage in Genesis 2 about God taking the two, male and female, and making them into one flesh, he called it a *mystery*. By this, he did not mean it was something confusing or hard to understand. He meant that something was previously hidden and it has now been revealed. What is revealed is that this unity of diversity of male and female is meant to be a testimony to the world about God. It is showing people the nature of how Jesus Christ, the Son of God, wants to unite with his people, the church. Marriage is not just for our joy but it is also a metaphor, parable, or symbol of something great and universal and eternal—the union of Christ with his bride. As we step into this marriage bond we become a living picture of God's wonderful union with his people. *Our unity tells a bigger story.* God is saying something to the world about his love for humanity in the way a husband and wife relate to each other. The love of a husband for his wife displays to the world the love Christ has for his church. The love of a wife for her husband communicates to the world how the people of God respond to Jesus. What exactly does that look like? Let's start with the ladies.

Everyone's Favorite Verb: Submit

In Ephesians 5:22 Paul stated, "Wives, submit to your own husbands, as to the Lord." Oh, what a fun verb! *Submit.* Everybody's favorite word. "What do you want to do today?" "Hmm. I don't know. Maybe, submit." I gathered a focus group of college students and asked the question, "When you hear the word *submit*, what comes to mind?" All the adjectives they used to explain it were intensely negative. I understand why. No one I have met initially loves the idea of submitting, myself included. On top of that, much harm has been perpetrated against women at the hands of domineering men. But before we prejudge this passage, we must gain clarity about what this word means in this context and what it does not mean. Let's begin by dispelling some misunderstanding.

Not Subjugation

When it says wives, submit to your husbands, submission does not mean subjugation. There is never a command for one human being to force another to submit in the Bible. You won't find a verse that says, "Husband, you get that woman to submit!" In the New Testament, the power to bring another into submission belongs to God alone. When the verb *submit* is used in this passage, it is used in what's called the *middle voice*. What middle voice means is that a person does the action of the verb to himself. In this instance, the wife submits herself. It's a decision a woman makes. This is a verse for the woman. She chooses to submit.[3]

Not Servitude

Submission is also not servitude. By this I mean that the passage does not suggest that women are second-class citizens. They are not intrinsically of less worth than men. They do not exist only to serve men. Paul was not suggesting when a husband marries he acquires a slave who must quietly obey his every whim. To submit does not mean to make yourself something less.

You may ask, "Then what *does* the word mean?" Let me give you the official definition. It means to order yourself under another. The verb submit carries the idea of subordination of one in an ordered array beneath another who has authority.[4] This idea also appears later in Ephesians 5 when it says the husband is the head of the wife as Christ is the head of the church (v. 23). The man is put in that position of authority. What does that mean? A simple way to say it is that to submit means to recognize and respond to a husband's leadership.

Submission As Recognition

To submit means, first, I recognize that God has ordered the world in a certain way. In doing so, he has put some authority structures in place. For any institution to function, there must be some degree of organization. And within that system someone must carry the responsibility of leading and others must carry the responsibility of responding. The word *submit* is used several times in ancient Greek writings to refer to soldiers coming underneath someone who is a superior rank. That soldier is not constitutionally less valuable than his commanding officer. But he understands that to advance as a unit toward a common goal there must be some degree of organization. Thus, submission is not a statement about worth, value, or equality. Rather, submission is about organizational structure. It is the acknowledgment someone has been given responsibility that someone else must come under.

Jesus, in Luke 2, submitted to his parents. Was Jesus a second-class citizen, possessing less value or less abilities than his parents? No. He was the Son of God! Even as a child he displayed capabilities vastly superior to any possessed by his parents, Mary and Joseph. Nevertheless, he understood God has ordained that parents have a level of authority over children, so Jesus willfully submitted himself to them.

Peter used the same word in 1 Peter 2:13 to describe how citizens respond to government. You and I are not constitutionally of less worth than a senator, judge, police officer, or the president. You might be substantially more gifted, intelligent, attractive, or capable than many senators, governors, judges, and even presidents. Yet, it is understood government structures exist for society to function, so we submit ourselves to the governing powers.

It is the same in marriage. As a wife, a woman recognizes God has placed the burden of responsibility upon a man to guide and care for his wife. The wife acknowledges this is a responsibility for which God will hold him accountable. Therefore, submission begins by recognizing that God has given a certain role and responsibility to husbands. But it does not end here. Godly submission does not simply passively acquiesce to God's design. Rather, the wife recognizes God's order and responds enthusiastically to both God and her husband within this structure.

Submission As Response

What does responding to a husband's leadership look like? I would say submission for a wife is an inclination to receive and affirm her husband's leadership.

I like the word *inclination* because it speaks to a general disposition or posture. I also like it because it clarifies that *submission* does not mean that a woman never initiates. Some people think that if a woman submits she must sit quietly and never voice her opinions, share her thoughts, or contribute ideas. She must simply wait for the man to come up with every thought. And even if she has a good idea that's obvious to everyone but her husband, she must sit there and wait for him to figure it out. But this is not the case. Read about the honorable wife in Proverbs 31. That woman is running a small business, buying and selling real estate. She is getting stuff done! Women *can* initiate and do many different things. However, the man bears the weight of responsibility to care for her. If he fails, God will take issue with him.

Therefore, whenever a man chooses to initiate and lead, his wife should be willing to receive that. She should hear him out and affirm him—letting him know that her general disposition is to respond positively to his efforts to lead.

Over and over again in my conversations with women, I hear them express the desire for a man who will take initiative. If you don't believe me, just put this in the context of dating. If you are a woman reading this, who would you rather go on a date with: A guy who asks you out, and then when you get in the car turns to you and asks, "So what do you want to do?" Or, would you rather go on a date with a guy who asks you out and when you get in the car he says, "Okay, I did a little research and I have picked two incredible restaurants. One of them is a great seafood place with a garden patio. The other one is a fantastic little mom-and-pop style Italian place. I do not know what you're in the mood for, so I kind of narrowed it down to two places that are both pretty amazing. What are you feeling?" When I presented this scenario in front of thousands of college students at Breakaway, the women in the arena erupted in applause for the second guy. Why? Because that is good leadership. He is initiating! I have not spoken to any woman who heard this and then responded, "Oh, two options? Are you trying to oppress me? Are you trying to hold me down? I'm sick of this!" Why not? Because good leadership does not feel like subjugation. Rather, it feels like freedom.

We will talk more about the responsibility of husbands in a moment. But ladies, I promise you want to marry a man who feels the responsibility to initiate on behalf of his wife and children. What is the greatest grievance against men in our country? That men do not feel the weight of responsibility to initiate on behalf of their family.

So much of the pain in the hearts of little girls comes from their dads never initiating to take them on dates when they were young. So much of the heartache of young men arises from their dads not initiating spending quality time with them. So much of the crime and societal problems in our country stems from men abandoning their wives and children. The selfishness and passivity of men has given rise to an incalculable amount of human suffering in our world. Ladies, you want a man who feels a sense of responsibility under God to care for his family. And when you see him doing his best to guide you and your kids in a good way, you want to let him know every way you can you affirm that!

When he says, "Hey, I think we should go to church," you should want to respond, "Yes! Let's do it." When he asks, "Hey, what if we tried to have a weekly date night, what do you think?" you reply, "That's a great idea. Thank you for doing that." As much as possible, you receive his leadership and affirm it.

Allow me to let you in on a secret, ladies: for many men, their biggest fear is to lead, because they are scared of failing. It is easier to numb out and watch TV than face the potential failure or rejection involved in making proactive decisions. Many of you have felt this fear if you have ever chosen to lead an organization. To stand in front of a group of people and declare, "We are going this way!" is a vulnerable place to be. If they don't follow you, you look like a fool. In the same way, when a husband takes the risk to initiate, and you affirm him, that breathes life into him. It promotes the pro-activity in men that so many women long for.

What I have discovered is that when single women express their concerns about submission to their husband's leadership, they speak about the fear of being micromanaged or of having their dreams crushed. But I would suggest to you that is not a fear of submission to leadership; that is a fear of submission to bad leadership.

Think about it in a work environment. If you have any kind of job, you must submit to the person you work for. What if an employer told you his goal is to crush his employees' dreams, destroy their goals, and rob them of their identity? Would you work for a company like that? No! That is a bad boss. Do not work for that guy. That style of leadership would be stifling.

But imagine you have a company with a boss who says, "Hey, I want to give you training to help you flourish and help you do what you are built to do. I want to give you resources to accomplish your goals. I am accountable to our board of directors to make this company as successful as possible in fulfilling our mission statement. I believe the best way to do that is to attract top talent and then position them to maximize their potential. So I'm going to work hard to figure out how to structure our organization and allocate our resources so that every person here feels freed up to use God-given abilities to accomplish substantive work that each person is passionate about." How would you respond to that boss? Would you ask, "How dare you attempt to be the boss of me!?" Probably not. You would love working there!

If you think that sounds fanciful, let me tell you, I worked at a place like this. My first job out of college was as a youth pastor at a brand-new church. The pastor was working hard to preach the Word of God, build a healthy organizational structure, and raise the funds we needed to reach our neighborhood for Christ. When it came to the youth department, his goal was to set me up to succeed. Whenever I met with him, he would ask me, "How can I help you?" He surrounded me with great resources, advice, and funding so that I could fulfill my role to the best of my ability. And when he saw gifts in me, he encouraged them and gave me room to grow and develop. I will be honest with you: though I would have said at the time that I hated the concept of submitting to someone, I loved working for that man. I knew he cared about me, and it was easy for me to support him and champion him as he led me. It was not oppressive to work for someone like that. It was freedom.

Leadership is not domination or enslavement. Submission is not neutering your mind or squelching your personality. An inclination toward receiving and affirming a husband's leadership does not mean that you do not initiate. It also does not mean that you do not speak your mind or at times disagree. What it does mean is that you are aware of his responsibility under God to carry the burden of leadership and affirm him every time he does it well.

If having a leader feels like oppression, let me implore you: pick the right leader! In Ephesians 5, Paul called women to submit "to your own husbands." In marriage, you are not signing up for submission to all men. You are vowing to respond to one man. This is why it is so important to pick the right man. Ladies, be discerning in dating. Don't settle for a selfish man and hope he will change. Get the right guy. Good leadership is a gift, not a burden.

It is also vital to choose a man who is worthy of your trust as well because, once you cross over into marriage, your relationship with God is now forever intimately bound up with this man. Ephesians 5:22 says, "Wives, submit to your own husbands, as to the Lord." What exactly does "as to the Lord" mean? I believe it means two things. First, it suggests *motivation*. It means that you submit to him as a function of your submission to the Lord. Your spiritual life under God is now forever bound up with this person. Your success as a worshipper will not primarily be determined by how many worship songs you sing or volunteer hours you serve. God ordained the leadership of the husband. If you receive and affirm your husband's leadership, you honor God by honoring the institution he made. If you are constantly critical or combative with your husband, you will dishonor the same God who created this institution.

It also speaks to *comparison*: you submit to your husband in the same way you submit to the Lord. That is no small statement. The passage goes on to say, "The husband is the head of the wife even as Christ is the head of the church, his body. . . . Now as the church submits to Christ, so also wives should submit in everything to their husbands" (vv. 23–24).

Now some people will ask, "In *everything*? What if he is doing something that is illegal?" Well, yes, there are caveats that, if he suggests you go kill some people, you should decline. Submission to husbands comes under the umbrella of submission to the Lord. Thus, you do not follow a husband into activity that expressly violates the commands of God. The reality is, however, we are often so quick to move to the caveats and minimize the weight of this statement: This man has a voice into every area of your life. That is big. Let that weight settle on you. Particularly if you are still in an unmarried season. Let the weight of this cause you to really evaluate whether or not you have the right guy.

For the married ladies, you are meant to submit to your husbands in the same way the church submits to Jesus. The church joyfully places itself under the loving headship of Jesus Christ. You will participate in God's picture to the world of how great a relationship with him can be when you affirm and respond to the leadership of your husband. Now every human husband will be imperfect. There will be aspects of his character or leadership or general disposition that you will wish was different. There will be ways you can lovingly call his attention to these things as you seek to both improve together. However, though there is much we could say on this topic, let me end with a call for you to focus on the positives. You will be a picture of the church's love for Christ as you joyfully receive and affirm your husband's leadership. One way to do that is to celebrate everything in his leadership that you can possibly celebrate. Look for the positives. Let him know when he has done something well. Do it without any backhanded dig like, "I really wish you would do that more often." Just let a pure compliment flow out to him. What is celebrated will be repeated. If he feels genuinely encouraged by you in a particular area, he will likely repeat that behavior. Avoid shaming him, particularly in front of other people.

I read a report recently that stated three out of four men say they would rather be respected than loved. Men desire respect more than all things and, interestingly, Paul called the wife to respect her husband. It is a way to encourage him—to meet him where he is—and be a blessing to him, the Lord, and to all those who desperately need to see a picture of how the church is to respond to her Bridegroom.

Now there is much more we could say, but let's now turn our attention to the men. There are forty-one words in the original Greek text to instruct the wife. There are 116 to educate the husbands. Wives are meant to submit to their husbands, but let's look specifically at what kind of man is worthy of a woman's submission.

Husbands Love

In Ephesians 5:25, Paul instructed husbands to "love your wives." That word translated "love" is the Greek term *agape*. It is not the Greek word *eros* from which we get the term *erotic*, meaning passionate, romantic love, though marriage is certainly meant to include this. It is not the term *storge*, which suggests familial affection—like you would have for a neighbor or a pet, though marriage should have this kind of warm affection. It is also not the word *philos*, which could be called a brotherly love, though we should certainly feel a deep friendship with our mate. While the word *agape* has a range of meaning, it is often used in Scripture to identify a higher love. A binding, covenantal love, like the kind of love God has for his people. It is a love that commits to the other's good and swears to never let go. You don't fall out of this kind of love. Passions can rise and fall. Agape stays. It declares to the beloved, "I'm not going anywhere." The verb *agape* is also in present tense in this passage. That suggests continuous action. That means a husband is meant to love his wife at all times and never stop.

So we know this love is meant to be present, active, and enduring. But what exactly does that look like? Paul continued, "as Christ loved the church" (v. 25). A man should love his wife in the same way Christ loves his church. How does Christ love his church? Paul told us, "[he] gave himself up for her" (v. 25).

In Greek, the single word we translate "gave himself up" is in the aorist tense, which suggests this verse is not necessarily pointing to the ongoing way Christ cares for his people. Rather, it points at one particular moment when Christ gave up his life for his bride on the cross. Gentlemen, do you want to know how you are supposed to treat your wife? Look at Jesus Christ on the cross. What did he do on that cross? Jesus Christ willingly sacrificed everything, down to the very last drop of his blood, to make her fully alive, as who she is meant to be under God. That is what Jesus did for his church. That is how a man is meant to love his wife. Ladies, I promise you it will be easy to follow a man who takes his cues from a God like that.

> **A husband's job is to initiate and sacrifice so that his wife might flourish under God.**

What does that look like on a practical level? Quite simply, a husband's job is to initiate and sacrifice so that his wife might flourish under God. This is what a man does.

A Man Initiates

Jesus did not wait to be asked before he came to earth to serve us, care for us, and die for us. He initiated. And how did his people look when he arrived? Was the church looking attractive? No! While we were sinners, Christ died for us. While we were at our worst, he gave his best. People who would eventually be a part of his church were the very ones driving nails into his hands. Jesus loved his people on their absolute worst day, while they were treating him like a joke or a villain.

How does a man love his wife? He is willing to sacrifice anything for her, even on her worst day when you get nothing back. That is how a man loves his wife. He will initiate to move toward her and sacrifice whatever he needs to sacrifice. And read in verses 26–27 why Christ did this for us:

> That he might sanctify her, having cleansed her by the washing of water with the word, so that he might present the church to himself in splendor, without spot or wrinkle or any such thing, that she might be holy and without blemish.

Jesus initiated. He moved toward us. He sacrificed, gave everything to protect and move sin out of the way. That is what sanctify means, that he is going to wash her clean. All the broken things and sad things, he is pushing them out of the way. He is taking the hit for sin for her so that she might be clean and pure. He protects.

Not only does he protect, he provides. Verses 28–30 explain, "In the same way husbands should love their wives as their own bodies. He who loves his wife loves himself. For no one ever hated his own flesh, but nourishes and cherishes it, just as Christ does the church, because we are members of his body." It says you are to take care of your wife like you take care of your body. You feed it, care for it, and make sure it is functioning. In the same way, you allocate resources however you must so that your body—your wife—might be cared for and operating at her fullest potential. You provide all she needs to be fully alive under God.

This is what Christ did for us, and this is what a man does for his wife. Husbands initiate and sacrifice so their wives can flourish under God. I think you see this idea clearly in the book of Genesis. Genesis 1 starts in a negative state. It says, "The earth was formless and void" (v. 2 NASB). Formless means it had no structure. Void means there was no content. It would be like saying there was no vase and no flowers filling the vase. No structure, and nothing to fill it. No form and no fullness. Yet, God initiated amid the chaos. In days one, two, and three, God created sea, air, and land. He formed the static life-support systems of the world. He created structure. Then, in days four, five, and six, he filled them with life, fish, birds, and animals. God created structure, but it is not a rigid, suffocating structure. It is structure that promotes life. Form that supports flourishing. Then when God created Adam, he told Adam to cultivate the ground. In this way, he was telling Adam to be God-like. What is cultivating? It is to structure an environment where the living things under your care can reach their maximum potential. That is what a man is meant to do in every sphere of life, and particularly in the home. Husbands initiate and sacrifice to create an environment where wives can flourish under God. Here's how:

1. *Initiate romance.* Plan dates. I remember when I was single and someone older would encourage us young men to continue to date our wives. We thought that was an unnecessary admonition. *Of course, we will go on dates*, we'd say to ourselves. But it is amazing once you get married how easy it becomes to get into a routine where the daily grind grounds out any romance. You both stumble home after a long day at work. One asks the other, "How was your day?" The response: "Exhausting." Then, the TV gets turned on and communication gets tuned out. You both start going to

bed when you are tired, wake up, and do it all over again. The next thing you know, you are functioning just like roommates and all the romance is gone. Men, you must fight back against this current of complacency. Initiate! Take her to a restaurant—preferably one without TVs so you can pay attention when she speaks. Write notes. Plan vacations. I have talked to many men who will say, as they contemplate divorce, "We just fell out of love." No, sir. You fell out of trying. Like any fire, the flames of romance must be tended to or they will grow cold. Stoke the flames.

2. *Initiate communication.* I had a seminary professor tell a group of us young men, "Never go to bed if you sense something is wrong with your girl. That may make for some long nights, and maybe a few sleepless ones, but joy will come in the morning." He then advised us that the way to make sure you do this is to initiate a time to pray together with your wife each night before you go to bed. The reason: it is hard to pray for each other when you are mad. If your prayer ends up sounding something like, "Lord, please smite my mate. Make them come to repentance," then you know there are some unresolved issues that need tending to. Initiating regular communication keeps little molehill-sized irritations from growing into mountainous marital problems.

3. *Initiate spiritual leadership.* Do not make your girl drag you to church. Be the initiator in getting the family going every Sunday. Read devotions with your family, especially if you have kids. Initiate conversations over dinner where you and your wife share what you are learning about God. Do not settle for just providing for your family physically and financially. Take up the role of caretaker of their emotional and spiritual health as well.

4. *Initiate sacrifice.* Embrace whatever inconveniences are necessary to ensure that you have created an environment where your wife can flourish under God. If the budget includes line items for all *your* technology and toys, but not for time for her to get a babysitter so she can spend life-giving time with friends, you need to rethink your financial strategy. If the hours you have together at the house include plenty of time for you to watch TV, but not enough time for regular face-to-face conversations, you may need to cut the cable. I know too many men who find the things they like to be "necessities," and the things she needs as "obligations" that may or may not make it into the budget. That is not sacrifice. If your "leadership" of your family always leads your family to the places where you get what you want and she does not get what helps her flourish, you are not being a Christlike leader.

I am not advocating being a servant to all her demands. But I am advocating being a student of all her needs. Study your wife. Continuously ask God, your wife, and yourself, "What does she need to help her be fully who she is meant to be under God?" Then do all you can to supply her with the time and resources to accomplish that end.

This is what Christ did on our behalf. When he created the world, he gave us a garden that was "pleasant to the sight and good for food" (Genesis 2:9). When we needed to hear from God, he sent prophets to speak to us. When we needed a perfect substitute, he lived the perfect life for us, embracing all the inconveniences of earthly life. When we needed forgiveness, he sacrificed his life to purchase our purity. When we needed hope beyond the grave, he defeated death for us. When we needed divine power for godliness, he sent his Spirit to enable us to live holy lives.

Jesus was watching us and saw what we needed and he provided it richly. That is what a husband does to provide for his wife under God. What helps her come alive? Is it time alone with the Word of God to study? How do I create that space for her? How do I give her time to leave the house? If a dirty house is confusing for her and she cannot focus, clean the house. Are there certain activities that make her come alive under God? Fund those activities.

* * *

I remember early in our marriage, I thought husbands had to build the furniture in the house because that is what men do. They build. So I would fight through the frustration and do my best to assemble a piece of furniture from IKEA. But my wife, Donna, would always watch me. Then she would slowly make her way over and begin to look at the instructions. She would pick up a few pieces and put them together. Then she would begin to take things out of my hands. Initially, I got really offended. *You think I can't build a desk? You think I'm not man enough to handle this?*

But over time, as I watched my wife, I realized that if you give her two hours she will start some kind of project. You give me two hours of free time, and I'm going to read a book. I realized that my wife loves to build things. One of the ways I could love her was to let her build! So one of my gifts to her for her birthday was a bunch of lumber. She built a picnic table in the backyard. Periodically, she will get another idea for something she would like to build: an end table or a headboard. I fund it. I am not a DIY guy, so I would never even think to try to build something myself that I could buy. But I know it makes my wife come alive, so I pay money for the materials she needs.

I am resolved to do whatever I have got to do, and create

whatever space I need to create to help my wife flourish under God. If she needs time away from the kids, we are going to pay for a babysitter. If she needs time to go meet with women who breathe life into her, I will stay home with the kids. I am going to sacrifice whatever time and energy I need to sacrifice so that she is fully herself under God.

Wayne Grudem, the author who wrote the book on biblical manhood and womanhood (entitled *Biblical Manhood and Womanhood*), was a successful seminary professor on the East Coast. But when he took his wife on vacation to Phoenix, Arizona, he noticed that the dry, desert air substantially improved her health. So he quit his job and moved to Phoenix Seminary, a little-known school at the time.[5] Why? Because that is what a man does. That is how a husband loves his wife. You initiate and sacrifice so she can be fully alive under God. Not to satisfy every whim or to be a prisoner to her every want and desire, but to provide the structure necessary so she can flourish as a woman made in the image of God. This is what Christ did for us, so we as men follow his lead and love our bride in the same way.

If you are single and not ready to love like that, then do not get married. If you are married, begin to serve like this, even if you do not feel that your spouse deserves it. We did not deserve grace, yet Jesus served us anyway. If there are ruptures or strains in your marriage, your servanthood may be the surest first step toward healing.

Marriage is a mutual commitment to lay down your life for the other person. This is what makes marriage both terrifying and fun. It can be scary to trust. For both men and women, when you marry someone, you surrender so much control in that moment. This other person could devastate you financially, ruin you socially, and cause deep emotional wounds. Your spouse could hold you back and hurt you tremendously.

Or, your spouse could be the best thing that ever happened to you. When each person enters the relationship as we have outlined above—with a resolve to serve and trust the other—marriage becomes much less fearful and much more wonderful. It is not a precursor for pain, but an amazing picture of the eternal love of God for us. So many young people I know are afraid of marriage because they are afraid of being hurt. But when you find someone who wants to honor God in every way they treat you, that crippling fear can be replaced with confident faith. You get to link up with an ally who you know will always have your back. I can truly say, more than a decade into marriage, that Donna and I have never been happier. I trust her. Serving each other has at times felt like a sacrifice, but the gain has been so much greater. We are better people and further along in life as a result of our commitment to love each other. And not only do we each have a great partner in life, but our partnership allows us to be a picture of the God we love so much. As a husband initiates and sacrifices, and a wife receives and responds to his leadership, the world gets to see a portrait of how Christ loves his bride, the church. This is the great joy in marriage. Our love for each other serves as an invitation for others to experience a love like this with the God who made them. We are safe in the arms of the One who sacrificed all for us. And when we lay down our autonomy in order to enter a relationship with him, we find that the great paradox is true: in losing our lives, we actually find them.

12

marriage as a pursuit

a case study // priscilla + aquila // acts 18

I had trouble sleeping in college. To help me doze off, I decided to have story time every night. My favorite series, by far, was The Chronicles of Narnia. If you have not read this masterful children's book series by C. S. Lewis, I encourage you to put my book down and go read them right away.

Go ahead.

I will be here when you get back.

If you have, then you know that Lewis packs profound spiritual and practical insights into entertaining stories about children who are called forth into adventure in the name of the great king, Aslan. In *The Voyage of the Dawn Treader*, the protagonist, King Caspian, assembles a crew to sail east into the unknown. Their mission is to rescue men from the kingdom who had been lost at sea, and then to continue on until they reach the shores of Aslan's land. While sailing across the vast sea, they encounter wild adventures, forge deep friendships, and participate in daring acts of rescue. It is then, in the midst of the mission, that Caspian meets a beautiful young woman, a daughter of the stars. They marry and she joins him on the *Dawn Treader* to continue their adventures together.

I remember lying in bed that night thinking, *Lord, that is what I want. I want to be a man who will venture forth into the purposes my King, Jesus, has for me. And if marriage be your will for me, then Lord, let us be a couple who will sail out on mission together.*

There are two great longings in the human heart: to belong and to matter. We want to be a part of a community that loves us and a cause that enraptures us. We want intimacy and we want impact. These great drives are woven deeply into the fabric of every human soul. And they are inseparably linked. In fact, what forges the deepest community on a sports team, within a company, or in a military unit, is the camaraderie that forms as a direct result of pursuing a common goal together. The same is true for a marriage.

Marriage is a team. It is a partnership; A union. Your marriage will only be as strong as your mutual commitment to a common vision.

In the previous chapter, we spoke about the values that should shape our marriages. Namely, husbands and wives should treat one another in the same way Christ and the church treat each other. When these values are reflected in a marriage, they provide for the world a picture of how Christ relates to his church.

However, in my experience, this is often where the discussion of Christian marriage ends. But this is not the end! Ephesians 5 is a wonderful presentation of the values that should shape a marriage. Yet there is little mentioned about what the husband and wife are meant to do together as they approach the world. Where are we meant to go as we love each other sacrificially? What mission are we meant to accomplish as we encourage each other? To end the conversation without discussing a shared purpose is like investing in a military unit's morale but giving it no mission. At some point we have to get this outfit moving. Marriage is the same way.

We are not meant simply to stare into each other's eyes. We are meant to link arms and run together after a common mission. C. S. Lewis's observation on friendship applies well to marriage: "The very condition of having Friends is that we should want something else besides Friends . . . Friendship must be about something . . . Those who have nothing can share nothing; those who are going nowhere can have no fellow-travellers."[1] The strongest marriages are those in which the husband and wife are truly friends. As friends they grasp each other's hand and run together after a common mission. And the more compelling the vision, the stronger the bond. In marriage we grab the hand of the other and run out into the world together to fulfill our God-given mission. In this way, marriage is not only a picture of Christ and his church to the world, it is also a pursuit of Christ's vision for the world. Your marriage will be most fulfilling and most secure when it is on mission.

> **Your marriage will only be as strong as your mutual commitment to a common vision.**

The Model Marriage

Here's some great news: the Bible provides us with a beautiful picture of what a married couple on mission looks like. Their names are Priscilla and Aquila, and the way they leveraged their marriage for the mission of God not only impacted the world back then but also still impacts our lives today.

We first meet this couple in the book of Acts. The latter half of the book of Acts focuses primarily on the missionary work of the apostle Paul as he and his team spread the gospel throughout the Roman Empire. In chapter 18, Paul is in the middle of his second missionary journey, having just left Athens and arrived in Corinth. It is here that he meets this remarkable couple.

> After this Paul left Athens and went to Corinth. And he found a Jew named Aquila, a native of Pontus, recently come from Italy with his wife Priscilla, because Claudius had commanded all the Jews to leave Rome. (vv. 1–2)

While in Corinth, Paul meets Aquila and Priscilla, who had just left their home in Rome because the emperor had commanded that all Jews depart from the capital city. Extrabiblical writings about this sweeping move from Rome's leader exist. The historian Suetonius wrote, "Claudius banished from Rome all the Jews, who were continually making disturbances at the instigation of one Chrestus."[2] Many New Testament scholars believe this is one of the first mentions of Jesus by an extrabiblical source. Here, Suetonius seems to get the word Christos (the Greek word for "Christ" or "the anointed one") confused with the name Chrestus (a common slave name). Claudius made this bold decision in AD 53, in the midst of the expansion of the gospel. Apparently, as it had done in many other cities, the arrival of the gospel in the city of Rome created great unrest among the Jewish population, who argued over whether or not Jesus was truly the Christ anticipated by the Old Testament. Much of the book of Acts records this same drama in other cities. In response, the emperor made the sweeping decision to simply cast out all Jews from the city of Rome.

Aquila and Priscilla arrived in Corinth, a large city that sat at the junction of major sea and land routes. There they set up a business. They were leatherworkers. Specifically, they made tents. Somehow Paul heard about them, and as he arrived in the city, he decided to go and see them. Now do not miss what is happening here: they had arrived because of government persecution stemming from the message of Jesus. And when they set up shop in their new town, here comes Paul, the guy who has been causing civil unrest across the Mediterranean as he unashamedly preaches the message of Jesus as the Christ. So how would Aquila and Priscilla receive him?

> He went to see them, and because he was of the same trade he stayed with them and worked, for they were tentmakers by trade. And he reasoned in the synagogue every Sabbath, and tried to persuade Jews and Greeks. (vv. 2–4)

Paul paid them a visit and they let him move in! They made tents together, and then Paul would go out every Sabbath and try to persuade Jews and Greeks that Jesus was the Christ. We find out later he had great success.

> And he stayed a year and six months, teaching the word of God among them. (v. 11)

For a year and a half Aquila and Priscilla's home became Paul's base of operations from which he continued his missionary work. Why would they take a risk like this? Because, as a married couple, they were committed to the mission of Jesus, and they were willing to leverage their work life and their home life for gospel expansion. In short, they were hospitable. This is the first of three characteristics demonstrated by Aquila and Priscilla's union that we will outline in this case study which will provide you with a vision of what a marriage on mission looks like.

Hospitable

It is important to note here that hospitality is far more than just giving a few dollars to a good cause every once in a while. Some of you may be doing that, yet your marriage possesses none of the thrill of being on mission together. This is not a couple budgeting to give to a few good causes because they feel that they are supposed to. This is a family that has made the decision to leverage all of their lives for the greatest of all causes. We can know this because, for many, when times get hard or uncertain we pull back our generosity. During the uncertainty of moving to a new city and the chaos of the cost of association with Jesus, Aquila and Priscilla still used what they had to further the proclamation of the gospel.

They are a perfect picture of what the apostle Peter advocated in 1 Peter 4:9–11:

> Show hospitality to one another without grumbling. As each has received a gift, use it to serve one another, as good stewards of God's varied grace: whoever speaks, as one who speaks oracles of God; whoever serves, as one who serves by the strength that God supplies—in order that in everything God may be glorified through Jesus Christ. To him belong glory and dominion forever and ever. Amen.

I love this passage because Peter dismissed the lie that you must be a great preacher or leader to make a difference for the cause of Christ. Do you want God to be glorified through Jesus Christ? Then you can use *whatever you have been given* by God to serve others! That may look like speaking, but it may also look like serving. Both are legitimate and necessary. Aquila and Priscilla were not orators like Paul. But their willingness to offer what they did have—their home and their tent business—made it possible for Paul to establish a church in Corinth. You do not have to be brilliant, excessively talented, or wealthy. But you must be willing. For Aquila and Priscilla, their home, marriage, business, and normal everyday lives were places of ministry. A couple who understands that their marriage is on mission to elevate the name of Jesus will suddenly find that everything they have can be leveraged for this great goal.

As someone in vocational ministry for almost twenty years, I have had the privilege of meeting several families like this. When I first started out in ministry, a young couple, Mark and Barkley Loser, invited me to Sunday lunch at their home. I was in a new city and did not know anyone. They did not hesitate to have me over to get to know their family. For the next several years, if I ever needed a meal, help with my car, or just some adults to hang out with, they were there. They also took on the responsibility of leading small group Bible studies with junior high and high school students. Just starting out, they did not have much money, but they leveraged what they had—a home and intentional time—to make a difference. As the youth ministry grew, we had a number of couples who did not have high school or junior high age children host Bible studies in their homes. They did it simply because they wanted their living rooms to be a place of spiritual life for others.

There are many others I could share, but let me ask you: Do you welcome people into your home? Do you welcome new people into your friendship circles? Do you serve in any ministries that help people feel connected? Are you practicing hospitality? It is a virtue, and is a beautiful part of marriage. This couple is going to change the world from their living room. Will you?

Game

As was often the case when Paul brought the gospel to a new town, things got a little crazy. Paul was arrested. The synagogue leader was beaten by a mob because of his leniency with Paul. These were tough days. When Paul set sail, Aquila and Priscilla went with him. They arrived in Ephesus. Luke made a point to tell us Aquila and Priscilla stayed there while Paul made a quick run back to his home base in Antioch. Why mention this? We find out a few verses later.

> Now a Jew named Apollos, a native of Alexandria, came to Ephesus. He was an eloquent man, competent in the Scriptures. He had been instructed in the way of the Lord. And being fervent in spirit, he spoke and taught accurately the things concerning Jesus, though he knew only the baptism of John. (Acts 18:24–25)

Aquila and Priscilla have been placed in an awkward situation. They traveled to Ephesus with the apostle Paul, but he had left. Now they find themselves sitting in the synagogue listening to a talented, passionate preacher who had bad theology. What should they do? What do you do when you hear a guy who is popular and passionate, but off theologically? Post some clips of him on YouTube alongside the title "False Teacher in Ephesus"? Complain at lunch to their friends that the synagogue has changed and it is not authentic anymore? Whisper to one another, "If Paul was here he'd show that guy what's up"? The following verse tells us how Aquila and Priscilla did decide to respond:

> He began to speak boldly in the synagogue, but when Priscilla and Aquila heard him, they took him aside and explained to him the way of God more accurately. (v. 26)

Catch that. They did not wait for a "real minister" to show up to talk to this guy. They also did not whisper about him behind his back or criticize him to their peers. What do they do? They approach him personally and instruct him. Not only are they willing to leverage their home and their business for the gospel, but they see every situation they are in throughout the day as an opportunity for ministry. Rather than stepping back and saying, "Man, somebody should do something about this. I wish a real minister like Paul was here to talk to this guy," they ask themselves the question, "What can I do to be a part of the solution?" There is a word for that. It is called being *game*. For those who do not know, *game* can be used as an adjective, meaning "eager and willing to do something new and challenging."[3]

This is a natural outworking of viewing your marriage as on mission. They have totally absorbed the perspective Paul articulated to the Ephesians that "we are his workmanship, created in Christ Jesus for good works, which God prepared beforehand, that we should walk in them" (Ephesians 2:10). Whether it be while making a tent or attending a service, they understood that each day held good works for them to do that they were meant to walk into. When they heard Apollos teach inaccurately, they knew, *We have had the benefit of learning from the apostle Paul for the last two years; we need to go help this man.* So they took up the awkward task of confronting someone. But they did it in the most redemptive way possible. They did not try to humiliate him or shame him in public. Rather, they "took him aside," choosing the most discreet way to confront him. In short, they were bold enough to speak the truth, and loving enough to do it in a way that built Apollos up, rather than tear him down. We should strive to be people who see the needs around us with a readiness to privately help rather than publicly hate. This is such an exciting way to live life, knowing that your God has fused eternal purpose into our everyday encounters. Aquila and Priscilla had this perspective. We are meant to as well. The world needs more couples who understand that they are ministers to their communities. When they see a problem they ask, "How can I be a part of the solution?"

Our friends, the Binghams, are one of the greatest examples of this perspective that I know. Ryan Bingham volunteered for Breakaway, the college ministry on the campus of Texas A&M that I had the honor of leading for more than a decade. Every Tuesday night thousands of college students gather to worship together in the basketball arena on campus. Ryan led our prayer team. When he graduated, he stayed in town and worked for a construction company. After a year or so someone asked me, "Do you know why Ryan is hanging out at the Northside dorms on Tuesday nights?" I had no idea. The next time I saw Ryan I asked him about it. Turns out Ryan noticed while he was a student that, as he drove to the arena for Breakaway, he would pass thousands of students just hanging out at their dorms. After he graduated, he decided that he needed to do more than simply observe this phenomena. So each week he designated about an hour to go visit with the students at the Northside dorms who were not a part of Breakaway. He befriended them, heard their stories, and even shared meals with them. He would pray with them, tell them about the love of God manifest in Jesus, and help at times with their tangible needs. He would also consistently invite them to join him as he walked over to Reed Arena. Over the next several months, I would notice that it was not uncommon to see Ryan sitting on a park bench somewhere on campus visiting with students. It also was not uncommon to see him at Breakaway with a few students in tow who looked as though they had no idea what was going on there. Ryan saw a need and decided that he had the capacity to be a part of the solution.

Over the years, he began to volunteer with the crisis pregnancy center in town as well. The organization had several women volunteers willing and able to counsel the scared, often young, expectant mothers. But the boyfriends or husbands would often sit alone in the waiting room until the sessions were over. Ryan volunteered to counsel these young men. In time, he left the construction company and went on staff at the pregnancy center full-time. Meanwhile, his sweet wife, Emily, finished her degree and began her career as a schoolteacher. She chose one of the lowest-income schools in town. Day in and day out she would serve among an underserved part of the community. When a ministry started to try to help the young women who worked at the local strip club, Ryan and Emily were ready to serve. As Emily and other women would go in to pray with and counsel the girls in the club, Ryan would stand outside and befriend the bouncers. By the grace of God, the club closed down a few years later. While many celebrated its exit from town, others realized it would put fear and financial strain into the lives of the women who worked there. As you would come to expect by now, the Binghams were a part of the community that helped these women find jobs to allow them to provide for their families. I am so inspired by this way of living life. While earning a living, investing in their marriage, and spending time with friends, they were also serving men and women all around the community. They are humble, below-the-radar peacemakers, weaving the grace of God into the city in which they live. Stepping into the story of God each day through new and exciting opportunities, they are a force for good in their hometown because they are *game*—willing to be a part of whatever God might have for them.

When the responsibilities of marriage pile on, it may feel like a stunning loss of freedom that sucks the joy out of life. You can reach a place where you feel as though you are just doing the things you have to do. But the Binghams' perspective changes that. When you believe that every day God has good for you to step into, it infuses the mundane with meaning. Simply making tents can change the world and open up each day to new opportunities to see and engage the Apolloses of the world.

What is the result of this kind of life? For Aquila and Priscilla, their investment in Apollos had extraordinary results. A few verses later we are told that Apollos began to travel to other cities.

> And when he wished to cross to Achaia, the brothers encouraged him and wrote to the disciples to welcome him. When he arrived, he greatly helped those who through grace had believed, for he powerfully refuted the Jews in public, showing by the Scriptures that the Christ was Jesus. (Acts 18:27–28)

Apollos becomes a force for the gospel. Paul talked about him throughout his first letter to the Corinthians and even put Apollos's ministry on the same level as Paul's or Peter's. Though the crowds may not have known the names Aquila and Priscilla, they would never have heard the gospel without their investment in Apollos.

How about you? Do you see the needs in your neighborhood as threats to your comfort or as opportunities to touch eternity? What good might God be calling you toward as a couple today? Are you game?

Faithful

While we do not see Aquila and Priscilla in the narrative of Acts again, Paul mentioned them in three of his letters. He wrote to the Corinthians while in Ephesus around the years AD 55–56. He closed the letter saying,

> The churches of Asia send you greetings. Aquila and Prisca, together with the church in their house, send you hearty greetings in the Lord. (1 Corinthians 16:19)

As Paul wrote to those in Corinth, he included a greeting from the couple who joined him in the work in that city. Two things are worth noting here. First, in four of the other passages where Priscilla and Aquila are mentioned together, Priscilla's name comes first.[4] Yet here Paul alternated their names. Why? It is hard to say, but I believe it shows that they were both active players in the work of ministry. It was not one of them doing the work of ministry while the other hung out on the sidelines. They were partners. You and your spouse may not be partners at work, but you will be partners in ministry in life. We are meant to function as a team.

Second thing to notice: the church in Ephesus met in Aquila and Priscilla's house. Apparently, the tentmaking business is doing pretty well! They had a living situation that afforded them the opportunity to gather the church in their home, and they willingly did so. Here, a few years later, this couple continues to offer hospitality to the people of God.

They appear again a few years later, around AD 57, in Paul's letter to the Romans. He concluded by saying:

> Greet Prisca and Aquila, my fellow workers in Christ Jesus, who risked their necks for my life, to whom not only I give thanks but all the churches of the Gentiles give thanks as well. Greet also the church in their house. Greet my beloved Epaenetus, who was the first convert to Christ in Asia. (Romans 16:3–5)

There are a few things to notice here. First, note that here, as well as in the letter to the Corinthians, Paul used a different name to refer to Priscilla. He called her Prisca. This is a more formal pronunciation of her name. It appears Paul wanted to sound more official when he included her name in his correspondence. Priscilla is a diminutive form of the name. Spanish works this way. *Hermana* means "sister." *Hermanita* means "little sister." It can be used to explain that someone is younger or smaller, but it is also often included as a means of suggesting endearment. Luke, who wrote the book of Acts, and who was on the journey with Paul when he encountered the couple, called her Priscilla throughout the book. This suggests that in addition to being Paul and Luke's "fellow workers" in ministry, they were also their dear friends.

Notice something else. Paul mentioned that this couple risked their lives for his. This raises an interesting question: When did that happen? Paul did not say. It may have been when they left Corinth with him. Things were getting dangerous there when they departed. But Priscilla and Aquila also ministered alongside Paul for quite some time in Ephesus. In Acts 19 we are told that Paul's ministry in that city resulted in a riot that almost cost him his life. So maybe they did something in Ephesus to save him. We are not sure.

About ten years later (AD 66–67), Paul wrote the last letter from him that we have, 2 Timothy. Paul was in prison in Rome, and he was confident this imprisonment would end with his death. Therefore, he wrote to the next generation of pastors and his son in the ministry, Timothy, to strengthen him as he leads the church in Ephesus. Paul concluded this letter to his beloved son by saying:

Greet Prisca and Aquila, and the household of Onesiphorus. (4:19)

As Paul was anticipating the end of his ministry and life, he looked up and saw that this same couple, Priscilla and Aquila, were serving alongside his protégé. They were shoulder to shoulder with young Timothy. That is amazing. There is an apt word that sums up all that we see in this couple's life in these three passages: *faithful*. They were ready to serve with what they had at any moment, and they were still ready to serve more than a decade later. They were a faithful couple. You may change cities—they moved from Rome to Corinth, to Ephesus, to Rome, and back to Ephesus—but you never change missions. God calls people to different battle lines all the time, but we are all in the same fight—not against people, but for people. It is a spiritual battle to speak the truth in love to all who will hear. Prisca and Aquila were faithful to the end, and that is what we are meant to be. We should be willing to go wherever the Lord calls to be servants to whomever he wills as long as he would have us do it. This is what a marriage on mission looks like: faithful service to our great King until he calls us home.

Donna and I befriended a couple who recently made a big move of careers and cities. They exited a part of the country they knew well, a house they loved, and a career path they could have easily traveled to a comfortable retirement. Instead, they packed up and moved to a new city as part of a new venture by a church they felt called to. I asked them why they were willing to give up so much, especially at an age where some people might be slow-

> **Your marriage is safest when it is on mission.**

ing down. The husband replied, "We have a mission statement as a family: we will do hard things that truly matter with people we love. This new venture meets that criteria, so here we are." I love that. Donna and I want to live like this. We want to go wherever

God wants us to go to do whatever God wants us to do. We want to be right in the center of what God is doing until the day he calls us home. This may mean you invest faithfully in the town you live in now for forty more years. It may mean you cross oceans to be a part of what God is doing in a far-off place. But marriages on mission know that death is the finish line for those in the service of God. We do not quit caring for the people around us until the day he calls us home!

Your marriage is safest when it is on mission.

Our marriages are a *picture* of Christ's love for his church, and our marriages are a *pursuit* of Christ's purposes on earth. Our marriages are a *mural* and a *mission*. To the degree that we take up his *values* of loving one another while we pursue his *vision* of extending the fame of Jesus around the world for the good of all people, we will have strong, successful marriages.

I promise you, your marriage is safest when it is on mission. Nothing forges stronger bonds of love than a mutual commitment to a compelling mission.

Soldiers will often speak of missing the battlefield, which can baffle civilians. Why would you want to return to a place of warfare and the constant threat of death? Soliders explain how being on a clear mission with a small group of people—who you know are committed to the same cause and committed to you—brings an intense form of brotherhood and loyalty that is unmatched in civilian life. I believe the same is true in ministry. Pursuing the cause of Christ with the community of Christ brings with it the great joy of camaraderie that is often missing in normal work-day life. The mission is a glue that fuses friends together and also strengthens marriages. One of the greatest gifts I have in life is the knowledge that Donna is committed to the same Lord I am. Our mutual commitment to him continuously reinforces, reaffirms, and strengthens our commitment to each other. It also produces wonderful friendships between us and the fellow workers and friends whom we live among. Ministry has given us amazing friendships with wonderful people. There is nothing in the world quite like being a part of the greatest of all communities chasing the greatest of all causes!

* * *

At a particular moment in *The Voyage of the Dawn Treader*, the travelers encounter enough difficulty that they begin to ponder whether or not they should discontinue the journey. In one of my favorite scenes, Reepicheep, the swashbuckling little mouse, speaks up:

> While I can, I sail east with the *Dawn Treader*. When she fails me, I will paddle east in my coracle. When she sinks, I'll swim east with my four paws, and when I can swim no longer, if I've not reached Aslan's country or shot over the edge of the world in some vast cataract, I will sink with my nose to the sunrise.[5]

The community rallies around Reepicheep, supporting the same cause, and the adventure carries on. At that point in the story, I remember praying, *That is what I want. Until my ship breaks apart and I drown, I am sailing toward my true King, with my nose to the sunrise. That's the kind of man I'm going to be. And Lord, I trust that you'll bring a woman along that has the same vision that I do and we'll be on a mission together.* And he did in due time. It took me longer than all my close friends to marry. It may take a while for some of you as well, but I would not trade my wife, so waiting longer than you would like is absolutely worth it.

conclusion

Seeking God first is like locating the North Star. Without him, the skies go dark. When human beings severed ties with God in Genesis 3, you see in the following chapters of Genesis where young men die and women get exploited sexually. This has been the case throughout history. When a man does not submit to God, the next most God-like thing in his life assumes the role. Often that is himself. Then the pursuit of life becomes: What will bring me maximum pleasure? When men think like this, often women and children are exploited. Look around the world today where lawlessness reigns. Who suffers? Women and children. But the men suffer as well. To exploit human beings like this, they must first lose aspects of their humanity, namely, their concern for others. Their instincts to cherish and protect must be numbed or seared. In the end, they become less human. Ascend to the role of deity in your life and you actually lose your humanity. You become a wild animal controlled by lust. This does not make for a stable society. Nor does it make for a warm one. When the structures fall, humanity does not flourish.

And yet, the goods news is that the bright and morning star has come to illuminate our path. The God of love sent his Son that we might be filled with life. He is our Guide and our Captain. When Christ established his kingdom, something changed.

Women were drawn to Christianity in such large numbers that by AD 370 the Emperor Valentinian, an opponent of the movement, issued a written order demanding that Christian missionaries cease calling on the homes of pagan women.[1] Why were women so drawn to this countercultural movement? Because they were afforded far higher status than women in the rest of the Greco-Roman world.

Men in Rome held marriage in low esteem. Several ancient correspondences contain their laments about the hassle of caring for a woman.[2] Sex was widely available through prostitutes in the city and a loose morality in men. Why promise to care for one woman if I can have sex with many without any obligation?[3] When they did marry, they went for the young thirteen-year-old girls.[4] When they had female children, it was commonplace to destroy them.[5] Eventually the ratio of men to women became skewed. When men's sexuality goes unchecked, women and children lose. Ultimately, so do men and so does society.

Christianity grew in this environment at a rapid pace because it approached sexuality so differently. Women were honored. Men did not commit incest, or child marriage, or divorce, or promiscuity. They faithfully loved one woman, their wives. They also faithfully joined their wives in raising their young girls. Why did so many Romans flock to what had initially been seen as a dangerous cult? Because they saw in Christianity a way of navigating life, love, and sexuality that allowed all to flourish. Men, women, and children were happier and healthier. Families were places of life. Sexuality was governed by love, not lust. Women and men mutually honored one another.

In essence, what Paul proclaimed in Ephesians 5 came true in practice: loving marriages became a picture to the world of what commitment to a loving God is like. When we walk in wisdom, we flourish. When we let the Spirit of God guide, he leads us to pleasant places. This is my hope for you. Submit your singleness, your sexuality, your spouse, and your soul to the Lord Jesus Christ. He is a good guide. Trust him, and he will lead you in a good way. And not you alone. The people of God pursuing romance God's way become a beacon of hope to the wider world. Cultures change when the world sees the beauty of godly romance. For the sake of your soul, your spouse, and the wider culture, do not settle for anything less.

We can careen into the treacherous seas on our own, or we can surrender the helm to the One who can skillfully pilot us through life's tempestuous seas. So let's end this book where we began. I do not know what God has in store for you in dating or marriage. But let me plead with you: before you get a relationship with a guy or a girl right, it is essential you get a relationship with God right. He is your source of life. He is your source of love. He is your stability. He is the hero who came for you, fought for you, died for you, and rose for you so that you could have life. He is the One who builds a structure in which you succeed and a kingdom in which you flourish. If you learn to trust him, he will make you the kind of person you are meant to be, and the world will be better for it.

acknowledgments

When I consider all the people who have been part of this book becoming a reality, *acknowledge* seems like too small a word. I would much prefer to hug, applaud, and celebrate a host of people with far more words than this space will allow. The people below are worthy of extensive praise, love, and shameless admiration!

The Stuart family. My wife and three little crazies: Hannah, Sparrow, and Owen. I love you with all my heart. I have no greater joy in life than linking arms and racing into the wild on adventures with all of you. I pray that you will always walk in close communion with our Lord. And, if it be his will, you walk through life with spouses who love him as much as you do. Much love to my mom, brother, sister and their families—your lives inspired much of what is displayed on these pages.

My beloved Breakaway family. This book began as a series of sermons that were written because of my love and sincere burden for the thousands of students I had the privilege to walk with during your critical university moments. Ministering among you on the campus of Texas A&M will always be counted among the greatest joys of my life. This includes leading under our amazing board of directors, and alongside the incredible staff of Breakaway. I am forever grateful that I have had the honor of laboring shoulder to shoulder with you. I am excited to see all that the Lord has in store under the amazing leadership of Timothy Ateek. I also want to specifically thank Elizabeth Staggers who helped with research for this book.

To my Passion family. I am forever grateful for the guidance, belief, and friendship Donna and I have received from our pastors Louie and Shelley Giglio. We see God more clearly and believe in Jesus with greater strength because of your influence. Thank you for cutting the wake for so many, us included. And to the brothers and sisters in the house: it is an enormous privilege to be running this race together with all of you! I'm grateful to be a part of the house. Particular thanks are due to the Passion Publishing team: Kevin Marks for believing in me and guiding me through the process of turning a passion into these pages, and Alissa Roberts, Hoke Bryan, and Stephanie Sommer for introducing this resource to the world.

The team at W Publishing. I like you! Thank you for being savvy and sincere, fun to work with, and fantastic human beings.

To my mentors. Gregg Matte, Ken Werlein, and Tommy Nelson. Your sermons and wise advice formed me long before this book was crafted. I routinely thank God for you.

And finally, to the countless single, dating, engaged, and married friends who have surrounded and supported our marriage and our family. I wish I could list you all. Thank you for loving us. We love you and are so grateful for your influence.

notes

introduction

1. Mark Regnerus and Jeremy Uecker, *Premarital Sex in America: How Young Americans Meet, Mate, and Think About Marrying* (New York: Oxford University Press, 2011).
2. Wendy Wang and Kim Parker, "Record Share of Americans Have Never Married," Pew Research Center's Social & Demographic Trends Project, September 23, 2014, accessed July 5, 2017, http://www.pewsocialtrends.org/2014/09/24/record-share-of-americans-have-never-married/.
3. "Population Themes," United Nations, accessed July 5, 2017, http://www.un.org/en/development/desa/population/theme/marriage-unions/WMD2015.shtml.
4. Pew Research Report, "Record Share of Americans Have Never Married," drawing conclusions from U.S. Census data.
5. D'Vera Cohn, Jeffrey S. Passel, Wendy Wang, and Gretchen Livingston, "Barely Half of U.S. Adults Are Married—A Record Low," Pew Research Center's Social & Demographic Trends Project, December 14, 2011, accessed July 5, 2017, http://www.pewsocialtrends.org/2011/12/14/barely-half-of-u-s-adults-are-married-a-record-low/.
6. Philip Zimbardo and Nikita D. Coulombe, *The Demise of Guys: Why Boys Are Struggling and What We Can Do About It* (Amazon Digital Services, 2012), 52.
7. Regnerus and Uecker, *Premarital Sex in America*.
8. Kay Hymowitz, Jason Carroll, W. Bradford Wilcox, and Kelleen Kaye, "The Knot Yet Report," 2013, http://twentysomethingmarriage.org/in-brief/.

9. Aziz Ansari and Eric Klinenberg, *Modern Romance* (New York: Penguin, 2016), 14–15; quoting study by James H. S. Bossard, "Residential Propinquity as a Factor in Marriage Selection," *American Journal of Sociology*, 38, no.2 (1932):219–24.

10. Timothy Keller and Kathy Keller, *The Meaning of Marriage* (New York: Penguin, 2013), 31–32, quoting Ernest Becker; Ansari, *Modern Romance*, 24–25, quoting Esther Perel's TED Talk, "The Secret to Desire in a Long-Term Relationship."

11. Zimbardo and Coulombe, *The Demise of Guys*, 74–76.

12. Hymowitz et al., "The Knot Yet Report," http://twentysomethingmarriage.org/the-great-crossover/; Ezra Klein, "Nine Facts About Marriage and Childbirth in the United States," *Washington Post*, March 25, 2013, https://www.washingtonpost.com/news/wonk/wp/2013/03/25/nine-facts-about-marriage-and-childbirth-in-the-united-states/?utm_term=.88f032e7f6ce.

13. Centers for Disease Control and Prevention, "Unmarried Childbearing," 2015, https://www.cdc.gov/nchs/fastats/unmarried-childbearing.htm.

14. Gillian Mohney, "Rhode Island Finds Increase in STDs After Rise of Social Media Dating," ABC News, May 27, 2015, http://abcnews.go.com/Health/rhode-island-finds-increase-stds-rise-social-media/story?id=31339541.

15. Allie Bidwell, "College Freshmen Socialize Less, Feel Depressed More," *U.S. News*, February 6, 2015, https://www.usnews.com/news/blogs/data-mine/2015/02/06/college-freshmen-socialize-less-feel-depressed-more; https://www.heri.ucla.edu/monographs/TheAmericanFreshman2014.pdf.

16. Wade Goodwyn, "Amid Rising Concern About Addiction, Universities Focus on Recovery," March 15, 2015, http://www.npr.org/2015/03/15/393038598/amid-rising-concern-about-addiction-universities-focus-on-recovery; Mary Brophy Marcus, "Heroin Use in U.S. Reaches 'Alarming' 20-Year High," June 23, 2016, http://www.cbsnews.com/news/heroin-use-in-u-s-reaches-alarming-20-year-high/.

chapter 1: god, guys, & girls

1. It's a true story about my friend, but the usage of the story as an illustration was inspired by a similar illustration I heard Francis Chan share.

2. Zachary Cohen, "US Navy's Newest Stealth Destroyer Christened,"

June 20, 2016, http://www.cnn.com/2016/06/19/politics/
uss-monsoor-zumwalt-destroyer-christened/.

chapter 2: the purpose of singleness

1. Some debate exists between scholars on what exactly Paul meant
   when he referred to the "gift" from God that he enjoyed and wished
   for others. Is the gift the state of being single? Or is the gift an ability
   granted to an individual, allowing him or her to remain single for a
   long time without, in Paul's words, "burning with desire" for sex? In
   other words, is the "gift" the *season* of singleness or *a decreased desire*
   for marriage and, more specifically, for marital sex? The language
   allows for both, so it is difficult to feel certain on either option.
   What we can say with certainty, however, is that God has ordained
   singleness and that everyone will experience it for some duration of
   time in their lives. We can also say with certainty that God calls for
   his people to enjoy sexual intercourse only within the confines of
   marriage. Thus the season of singleness is meant to be accompanied
   by sexual chastity. When God ordains (gifts) a season of singleness
   in your life, God will supply (gift) you with the ability to be sustained
   in it. No one will say God put me in a season of life that he did not
   equip me for. God equips his people for the moments he puts us in.
   So in your single years, are you capable of remaining pure sexually
   and being fulfilled in the Lord absolutely? Yes. Is the ability to be
   single and not desire sexual intimacy a unique situation in life? Yes.
   It does appear that Paul was suggesting he possessed the ability
   to be single and sexually pure for a longer period of time. Some
   of you may experience this as well, and God may very well have
   equipped you with a lower drive for marital intimacy because he
   has purposes for you that are better served while you are single. But
   for every person whom God has ordained with singleness, he will
   provide for you and he'll provide you the grace you need to honor the
   commands he has given for sexual purity.
2. Gordon D. Fee, *The First Epistle to the Corinthians* (Grand Rapids, MI:
   William B. Eerdmans Publishing, 1987), 347.
3. *Merriam-Webster* Online, s.v. "appropriate," https://www.merriam-
   webster.com/dictionary/appropriate.
4. Augustine, *The Confessions of Saint Augustine*, Book 1 (Chicago: Moody
   Press, 1981).
5. Elisabeth Elliot, *Passion and Purity: Learning to Bring Your Love Life
   Under Christ's Control* (Revell, 2002), 80.

6. Zimbardo and Coulombe, *The Demise of Guys*, 10.

chapter 3: a singleness case study

1. African proverb.
2. Zimbardo and Coulombe, *The Demise of Guys*, 64.
3. http://www.centeronaddiction.org/newsroom/
   press-releases/2011-family-dinners-report-finds-teens-who-have-
   infrequent-family-dinners.
4. John Piper, *When I Don't Desire God* (Wheaton, IL: Crossway, 2004),
   129.
5. James B. Stewart, "Facebook Has 50 Minutes of Your Time Each Day.
   It Wants More.," *New York Times*, May 5, 2016, https://www.nytimes.
   com/2016/05/06/business/facebook-bends-the-rules-of-audience-
   engagement-to-its-advantage.html.
6. Corrie ten Boom, "Guideposts Classics: Corrie ten
   Boom on Forgiveness," *Guideposts*, July 24, 2014, https://
   www.guideposts.org/better-living/positive-living/
   guideposts-classics-corrie-ten-boom-on-forgiveness.
7. Elisabeth Elliot, *Shadow of the Almighty: The Life and Testament of Jim
   Elliot* (Grand Rapids, MI: Zondervan, 2009), 59.

chapter 4: who to date

1. Ansari and Klinenberg, *Modern Romance*, 96.
2. Ibid., 107.
3. Jonathan Grant, *Divine Sex: A Compelling Vision for Christian
   Relationships in a Hypersexualized Age* (Ada, MI: Brazos Press, 2015),
   150 (iBooks edition).
4. A. W. Tozer, *The Knowledge of the Holy: The Attributes of God* (San
   Francisco: Harper One, 2009).
5. Tommy Nelson, *Love Song: A Study in the Song of Solomon*. Denton
   Bible Church Media.
6. This definition is adapted from Tim Keller's excellent sermon series
   on the book of Proverbs.
7. George Sayer, *Jack: A Life of C. S. Lewis* (Wheaton, IL: Crossway
   Books, 1994), 389.

chapter 5: how to date

1. David Brooks, "The New Lone Rangers," *New York Times*, July 10,
   2007, http://www.nytimes.com/2007/07/10/opinion/10brooks.html.
2. Ansari and Klinenberg, *Modern Romance*, 34.

3. Helen Fisher, "Psychology of Love: Why We Love. Why We Cheat.," The Naked Convos, http://thenakedconvos.com/psychology-love-love-cheat/.

4. See Song of Solomon 8:4.

5. Ansari and Klinenberg, *Modern Romance*, 80–3.

chapter 6: sex

1. Amanda Lenhart, "Teens and Mobile Phones Over the Past Five Years: Pew Internet Looks Back," Pew Research Center, August 19, 2009, http://www.pewinternet.org/2009/08/19/teens-and-mobile-phones-over-the-past-five-years-pew-internet-looks-back/.

2. Amanda Lenhart, "Teens, Social Media & Technology Overview 2015," Pew Research Center, April 9, 2015, http://www.pewinternet.org/2015/04/09/teens-social-media-technology-2015/.

3. Kelly Wallace, "Half of Teens Think They're Addicted to Their Smartphones," CNN, updated July 29, 2016, http://www.cnn.com/2016/05/03/health/teens-cell-phone-addiction-parents/.

4. "Mobile Mindset Study," Lookout, 2012," https://www.mylookout.com/resources/reports/mobile-mindset.

5. Kelly Wallace, "Teens Spend a 'Mind-boggling' 9 Hours a Day Using Media, Report Says," CNN, updated November 3, 2015, http://www.cnn.com/2015/11/03/health/teens-tweens-media-screen-use-report/index.html; https://www.commonsensemedia.org/about-us/news/press-releases/landmark-report-us-teens-use-an-average-of-nine-hours-of-media-per-day.

6. http://www.npr.org/templates/transcript/transcript.php?storyId=439192407.

7. Alexis Kleinman, "Porn Sites Get More Visitors Each Month than Netflix, Amazon and Twitter Combined," Huffington Post, May 4, 2013, http://www.huffingtonpost.com/2013/05/03/internet-porn-stats_n_3187682.html.

8. Jason S. Carroll, Laura M. Padilla-Walker, Larry J. Nelson, Chad D. Olsen, Carolyn McNamara Barry, and Stephanie D. Madsen, "Generation XXX: Pornography Acceptance and Use among Emerging Adults," *Journal of Adolescent Research*, 23, (2008):6–30.

9. Regnerus and Uecker, *Premarital Sex in America*, kindle edition: 1840.

10. http://tedxnavesink.com/project/dr-gail-dines/.

11. American Psychological Association, "Sexualization of Girls," http://www.apa.org/pi/women/programs/girls/report.aspx.

12. David Finkelhor, Gerald Hotaling, I. A. Lewis, and Christine Smith,

"Sexual Abuse in a National Survey of Adult Men and Women: Prevalence, Characteristics, and Risk Factors," *Child Abuse and Neglect*, 14, no. 1 (1990): 19–28.

13. Grant, *Divine Sex*, 186.
14. Ibid., 198; quoting survey: Dolf Zillmann, "Influence of Unrestricted Access to Erotica on Adolescents' and Young Adults' Dispositions toward Sexuality," *Journal of Adolescent Health*, 27, no. 2 (2000): 41–44.
15. Zimbardo and Coulombe, *The Demise of Guys*, 14–15.
16. Grant, *Divine Sex*, 68.
17. Regnerus and Uecker, *Premarital Sex*, 191–92.
18. Regnerus and Uecker, *Premarital Sex*, ebook: 2776–2809.
19. Grant, *Divine Sex*, 182–183, quoting Norman Doidge, "Acquiring Tastes and Loves," *The Brain That Changes Itself: Stories of Personal Triumph from the Frontiers of Brain Science*, 107.
20. Regnerus and Uecker, *Premarital Sex*, ebook: 2983.
21. Grant, *Divine Sex*, 187, quoting Doidge, "Acquiring Tastes and Loves," 104.
22. Naomi Wolf, "The Porn Myth," *The New Yorker*, accessed May 24, 2004, http://nymag.com/nymetro/news/trends/n_9437/.
23. Donna Freitas, presentation at the Q Conference, Qideas.org/videos/hookup-culture/.
24. Ibid.
25. Patrick Carnes, *Out of the Shadows* (Hazeldon Information & Educational Services, 2001), 152.

chapter 8: how to know that you know
1. Robert R. Perkinson, *Chemical Dependency Counseling: A Practical Guide* (Thousand Oaks, CA: SAGE Publications, 2017).

chapter 9: becoming one
1. Kelly Holland, "Fighting with Your Spouse? It's Probably About This," CNBC, February 4, 2015, http://www.cnbc.com/2015/02/04/money-is-the-leading-cause-of-stress-in-relationships.html.

chapter 11: marriage as a picture
1. Katie Benner, "Apple iPhone 6s Breaks First-Weekend Sales Record," *New York Times*, September 28, 2015, https://www.nytimes.com/2015/09/29/technology/personaltech/apple-iphone-6s-breaks-first-weekend-sales-record.html.
2. W. Bradford Wilcox and Elizabeth Williamson, "The Cultural

Contradictions of Mainline Family Ideology and Practice," *American Religions and the Family*, edited by Don S. Browning and David A. Clairmont (New York: Columbia University Press, 2007), 50.

3. Harold W. Hoehner, *Ephesians: An Exegetical Commentary* (Ada, MI: Baker Academic, 2002),717, 731–732, 745; Peter T. O'Brien, *The Letter to the Ephesians* (Grand Rapids, MI: William B. Eerdmans Publishing, 1999), 411.

4. Hoehner, *Ephesians*, 716; O'Brien, *The Letter to the Ephesians*, 399.

5. Wayne Grudem, "Upon Leaving: Thoughts on Marriage and Ministry," *Trinity Magazine*, 2001, http://www.waynegrudem.com/wp-content/uploads/2012/03/Upon-Leaving-Thoughts-on-Marriage-Ministry1.pdf.

chapter 12: marriage as a pursuit

1. C. S. Lewis, *The Four Loves* (New York: Harcourt Books, 1971), 79–80.

2. Gaius Suetonius Tranquillus, *The Lives of the Twelve Caesars, Volume 05: Claudius* (FQ Books, 2010), 25.4.

3. *Merriam-Webster* Online, s.v. "game," https://www.merriam-webster.com/dictionary/game.

4. Fee, *The First Epistle to the Corinthians*.

5. C. S. Lewis, *The Voyage of the Dawn Treader* (New York: Harper Collins, 1994).

conclusion

1. Rodney Stark, *The Rise of Christianity: How the Obscure, Marginal Jesus Movement Became the Dominant Religious Force in the Western World in a Few Centuries* (Harper San Francisco, 1997), 95.

2. Ibid., 117.

3. Ibid.

4. Ibid., 106.

5. Ibid., 118.